KEY ISSUES IN SECONDARY EDUCATION

Also available from Cassell:

John Beck: *Morality and Citizenship in Education*
Asher Cashdan and Lyn Overall (eds): *Teaching in Primary Schools*
L. B. Curzon: *Teaching in Further Education*
Andrew Pollard and Pat Triggs: *Reflective Teaching in Secondary Education*
John Wilson: *Key Issues in Education and Training*

Key Issues in Secondary Education

Introductory Readings

Edited by
John Beck and Mary Earl

CASSELL
London and New York

Cassell

Wellington House
125 Strand
London WC2R 0BB

370 Lexington Avenue
New York
NY 10017–6550

First published 2000

British Library Cataloguing-in-Publication Data
A catalogue record for this book is available from the British Library.

ISBN   0-304-70557-8 (hardback)
        0-304-70558-6 (paperback)

Typeset by Kenneth Burnley, Wirral, Cheshire.
Printed and bound in Great Britain by Biddles Ltd, Guildford and King's Lynn.

Contents

Preface

After a few weeks of their initial training course, when trainee teachers come together in inter-disciplinary groups to share their observations and experiences in differing schools, their perspectives are varied and wide ranging, and their questions challenging:

- '*Your* school seems to have a much wider option choice for pupils in Years 10 and 11 than *mine;* how does it manage to do that, within the constraints of the National Curriculum?'
- 'Mixed-ability teaching is central to the ethos of *my* school; how does *your* school try to ensure that setting doesn't restrict opportunity and affect teacher expectations?'
- 'On my second day, I had a chance to take part in this brilliant staff development session on teaching and learning strategies across all subjects; it was excellent listening to teachers who *really* wanted to exchange and develop good practice!'
- 'The Head said there wasn't a gender gap at GCSE, but when I asked in the department, they didn't seem to know if there was or not in my subject.'
- 'I'm to shadow a tutor next term; I don't know, I find the pastoral side really scary! I don't know anything about ...'
- 'I spent the morning at one of the local primary schools; it was fascinating hearing why most of their pupils opt to go to *my* school rather than the other one in the town.'

Once the observations start, the flow can be ceaseless, as trainees gain strength and reassurance by sharing experiences and examining their own preconceptions and their own schooling. This book has evolved from the Readings which support the Core Studies course in the University of Cambridge Faculty of Education secondary postgraduate course. The chapters address the crucial cross-curricular issues which are central to secondary schooling at the turn of the century (and the beginning of a new millennium), and they incorporate ideas and strategies developed in conjunction with a wide number of partnership secondary schools. We are confident that the views expressed in this volume will make a major contribution to the understanding of young (and not-so-young) new teachers, as they grapple with issues which go beyond subject boundaries, and as they explore fundamental issues which affect schools and young people today.

PROFESSOR DONALD MCINTYRE
Head of the School of Education
University of Cambridge

MICHAEL YOUNGER
Director of Postgraduate Courses
University of Cambridge Faculty of Education

About the Contributors

Madeleine Arnot is University Lecturer in Education in the School of Education, University of Cambridge, and a Fellow of Jesus College. Her teaching and research interests lie in the sociology of education, especially in relation to issues of gender, social class, 'race' and citizenship. Recent publications include *Recent Research on Gender and Educational Performance* with J. Gray, M. James and J. Rudduck (OFSTED/Stationery Office 1998) and *Closing the Gender Gap: Post-war Education and Social Change* with M. David and G. Wiener (Polity 1999). She is an executive member of the editorial boards of *International Studies in Sociology of Education*, *The British Journal of Sociology of Education*, and is an international consultant for *Gender and Education*.

John Beck teaches sociology of education and curriculum and professional studies. He is Head of Education Studies at Homerton College, Cambridge. His research interests include values education, political and citizenship education, and personal and social education. He is author of *Morality and Citizenship in Education* (Cassell 1998).

Gabrielle Cliff Hodges was formerly Head of English in a Cambridgeshire comprehensive school and is now Secondary Team Leader at Homerton College, Cambridge. She jointly co-ordinates the secondary English and Drama PGCE course and lectures in English, language, children's literature and professional studies. She has contributed chapters about speaking and listening and poetry to *Learning to Teach English in the Secondary School* (1997) and about reading to *Where Texts and Children Meet* (forthcoming) and *Issues in English Teaching* (forthcoming). She is also co-editor of, and contributor to, *Critical Narratives: Tales, Tellers and Texts* (1999). From 1996 to 1998 she was Chair of the National Association for the Teaching of English.

Mary Earl is Senior Lecturer in Religious Studies at Homerton College, Cambridge. She was formerly Head of RE at a Hertfordshire comprehensive school and then at a Cambridgeshire sixth-form College. She has also worked both at school and higher education level as a trainer and consultant in PSHE areas of the curriculum. Research interests include A-level teaching of world religions; spirituality and psychology; and narrative and the development of values. Publications include 'Narrative and the development of values' in E. Bearne (ed.) *Language Across the Secondary Curriculum* (1990).

Philip Gardner lectures in the University of Cambridge School of Education where he specializes in history of education and has particular research interests in the development of the teaching profession in the nineteenth and twentieth centuries. His most recent publication in this field is 'Classroom teachers and educational change 1876–1996', *Journal of Education for Teaching,* 24 (1). With Peter Cunningham of Homerton College, Cambridge, he is currently working on a number of research projects using oral history as a principal method.

Ruth Joyce is now in charge of the Drug Prevention Unit of the Home Office Drug Prevention Office based in Bristol. She was previously Head of Education for Prevention at SCODA (the Standing Conference on Drug Abuse) and, before that, Drug Education Adviser for Cambridgeshire LEA. She has been a regular contributor to the University of Cambridge PGCE programme, updating trainees annually on current developments in drug education nationally.

Terence H. McLaughlin is University Lecturer in Education in the University of Cambridge and Fellow of St Edmund's College, Cambridge. He specializes in philosophy of education and has published widely on many aspects of the field. He has taught English and been Head of Year and Head of Sixth Form in two comprehensive schools, and is currently Vice-Chair of the Philosophy of Education Society of Great Britain. He has recently edited (with Mark Halstead) *Education in Morality* (1998), a collection of papers on philosophical aspects of moral education.

John Raffan is a lecturer in the University of Cambridge School of Education, with particular responsibility for Science/Chemistry Education. He has been involved with curriculum development and evaluation for several large-scale national projects and with assessment as an examiner for Awarding Bodies (Examination Boards) and as a consultant with the Qualifications and Curriculum Authority and its predecessors. His recent publications include: *Foundation Chemistry* with B. Ratcliff (1995); 'Industry-linked projects in science education', in W. C. Beasley (ed.) *Chemistry: Expanding the Boundaries* (1996); and *A Pilot Study Evaluation of UK Co-ordinated Socrates: Comenius Action 1 School-based Partnership Programmes,* with A. Adams and M. Evans, University of Cambridge School of Education (1996).

Michael Reiss is Reader in Education and Bioethics at Homerton College, Cambridge, a priest of the Church of England and an accredited counsellor. He was a member of the Cambridgeshire LEA Working Group that produced the County's Sex Education Guidelines in 1992 and has acted as a consultant on sex education and/or values to a number of governments and organizations. Recent publications in the field of sex education include: *Sex Education and Religion* (Reiss and Mabud 1998); 'Teaching about homosexuality and heterosexuality', *Journal of Moral Education,* 26, (1997), pp. 343–52; 'Food, smoking and sex: values in health education', in J. M. and M. J. Taylor (eds) *Values in Education and Education in Values,* (1996, pp. 92–103).

Martyn Rouse is a specialist in the field of special educational needs; he teaches at the University of Cambridge School of Education. He has undertaken commissioned research for local authorities into the development of inclusive schools in the UK. Recently he carried out research on the impact of school reform on the education of children with special needs for the US Department of Education in association with a consortium of US universities. Other research interests include the evaluation of special education policies and the assessment of students with special needs. He has published extensively on a wide range of issues in the areas of special educational needs and inclusive education. His recent publications include *School Reform and Special Education Needs: Anglo-American Perspectives* (co-edited with L. Florian) and *Special Education and School Reform in Britain and the United States* (with M. McLaughlin) (in press).

Kenneth Ruthven taught in Scotland and England before joining the University of Cambridge School of Education where he is Reader in Education. His own thoughts on assessment can be found in 'Better judgement: rethinking mathematics education', *Education in Mathematics,* 27, 4, (1994), pp. 433–450 and in 'Beyond common sense: reconceptualising National Curriculum assessment', *The Curriculum Journal,* 6, 1, (1995), pp. 5–28.

Chris Tubb lectures in Education Studies at Homerton College, Cambridge. She teaches philosophy of education and also contributes to curriculum and professional studies courses for both undergraduate and PGCE students. Her research interests include moral and values education, and she is particularly interested in the morality of war and just war theory.

Rex Walford is University Lecturer in Education in the School of Education in the University of Cambridge and a Fellow of Wolfson College, Cambridge. He has particular interests in experiential learning in classrooms and has written several books about the use of simulation and game techniques. His latest book is a history of geographical education in Britain, due to be published early in 2000. He is director of the research phase of the Land Use–UK project, which has involved over 1,500 schools in mapping and commenting about their local environments.

Angela Webster is Senior Manager/Head of Key Stage 4 and Professional Tutor for initial teacher education and training at Parkside Community College, Cambridge, and a former Head of Geography at schools in Cambridgeshire and Sheffield. Recently seconded to Homerton College as Secondary Subject Lecturer for Geography, she has written extensively on teaching styles and enquiry-based learning, and on issues of assessment in geography.

Michael Younger is Director of Postgraduate Courses within the University of Cambridge Faculty of Education and is based at Homerton College. He has co-authored, with Molly Warrington, a series of papers on perspectives on the gender gap in secondary schools in England and Wales, the most recent being published in *British Journal of Sociology of Education,* 20, 3, (1999); *Research Papers in Education,* 14, 1, (1999); and *British Educational Research Journal,* 25, 5, (1999). He is currently researching on single-sex teaching within mixed comprehensive schools. Other interests include environmental education and the changing nature of secondary Initial Teacher Training partnerships.

Introduction

This book concerns the work of secondary schools. It is primarily addressed to teachers in training and to those in their induction year, though the issues it discusses are of significance for all who teach in secondary schools. Teacher training has undergone extensive reform in recent years, much of it, rightly, focused upon raising the quality of subject teaching. Subject teaching, however, is far from being the whole of teaching. All who work in schools share a set of wider concerns and responsibilities, to do with the education of the whole child or young person. Although discussion of this broader dimension of education can all too easily become either platitudinous or polarized around false dichotomies, the issues involved are of central importance – both for schools and for society as a whole.

Since at least the 1970s, schools and teachers have been recurrently blamed for many of society's problems – or perceived problems. Politicians, media pundits, 'think tanks' of both the right and the left, and many others have repeatedly attacked schools, and more particularly comprehensive schools, for 'failing to deliver' on a whole range of issues (see Beck 1998). At various times, schools and teachers have been held responsible for alleged national decline in a wide diversity of areas: for falling academic standards (e.g. Cox and Dyson 1969); for national industrial decline and subverting the values of enterprise culture (e.g. Weinstock 1976); for promoting relativistic moral beliefs and undermining traditional moral values and religion (e.g. Norman 1977, The Hillgate Group 1986); for promoting multiculturalism at the expense of Britain's cultural heritage (e.g. Scruton 1987). The election of a 'New Labour' government in 1997 did not stem this tide of criticism, though its content changed. School effectiveness and raising standards became the dominant preoccupations, with concomitant 'naming and blaming' of failing institutions and recurrent exhortations to teachers to raise their expectations of pupils to ever higher levels.

In an image-conscious age, there can be little doubt that recurrent criticism of this kind has damaged the image of teaching in the public mind and lowered its appeal to many young people (though this is far from being the only reason for difficulties of teacher recruitment in recent years). All this is unfortunate. Arguably, schools and teachers have major *achievements* to their credit. For example, our society is probably significantly more tolerant and less racist than it was 30 or 40 years ago (even if there is still a considerable distance to travel); more people are better informed and more concerned about the environment; and such progressive attitudes are probably more common among younger age groups in the population. Although direct cause-and-effect relationships can never be demonstrated in areas of this kind, it is hard to believe that educational institutions played no significant part. Schools alone cannot 'make people good' or turn them into good citizens. But the role of schools in personal, moral, spiritual and social education remains vitally important and its contribution should be neither neglected nor unfairly disparaged.

This book originated as an 'in-house' set of readings written for initial teacher training students taking the secondary Postgraduate Certificate in Education in the University of Cambridge School of Education and at Homerton College. Like most such courses, this PGCE programme contains a substantial element of General Professional Studies, taken by all trainees alongside their main subject work. The main aim of such courses, and of this book, is to introduce student teachers to a range of issues which are of decisive importance for the general professional development of all teachers in the secondary phase, irrespective of their subject specialisms, including helping trainees to develop their understanding of a range of *value-related issues* which are inescapably associated with the personal, moral, spiritual and social development of young people. Government regulations now specify a series of 'Other Professional Requirements' which all teachers must know about if they are to achieve Qualified Teacher Status; these are set out in Annex A, Section D of Circular 4/98 (DfEE 1998). Included here are topics such as: teachers' legal liabilities and responsibilities, teachers' conditions of service, child protection, school governing bodies, etc. (see Cole 1999).

Even more recently, a powerful impetus has been given to cross-curricular innovation in these non-subject-specific areas of the curriculum as a result of the publication in May 1999 of a government consultation document setting out proposals for further revision of the National Curriculum in England, to take effect from September 2000 onwards. The proposed revisions include the introduction of a non-statutory framework for the teaching of Personal, Social and Health Education (PSHE) in all four Key Stages, and for the introduction from 2002 of Citizenship Education as a new Foundation Subject at Key Stages 3 and 4 only (QCA and DfEE 1999). The way in which government sees the key issues in this area of the curriculum as being strongly inter-related is made clear in the following extract from the draft statutory order for this 'proposed new foundation subject for citizenship':

Citizenship contributes to the school curriculum by giving pupils the knowledge, understanding and skills to enable them to participate in society as active citizens of our democracy. It enables them to be informed, critical and responsible and aware of their duties and rights. Within a school framework which also promotes the social, moral and cultural development of pupils it promotes their personal and social development, enabling them to become more self-confident and responsible in and beyond the classroom. It is complemented by the non-statutory framework for personal, social and health education at key stages 3 and 4. Citizenship encourages pupils to become helpfully involved in the life of their schools, neighbourhoods, communities and the wider world. It promotes their political and economic literacy through learning about our economy and our democratic institutions, with respect for its varying national, religious and ethnic identities. It helps them to gain a disposition for reflective discussion. It shows pupils how to make themselves effective in the life of the nation, locally, regionally, nationally and internationally. (*ibid.* p. 28)

It is important to recognize that not only are many of the specific issues identified here ones which involve significant controversy, but also that the whole idea that schools should seek to get formally involved in matters of this kind is itself controversial. For example, as soon as the proposals for the PSHE framework and citizenship education were announced, they were vigorously attacked by some sections of the press. The *Daily Mail,* under a front page headline 'Labour drop marriage from morality classes for children', attacked the PSHE proposals because they contained 'not a word about marriage' and because they 'do not mention the traditional two-parent family either' (*Daily Mail* 1999, p. 1). In the same newspaper, Professor Anthony O'Hear launched an uncompromising attack on the citizenship education proposals:

The Government is about to introduce lessons in citizenship as part of the National Curriculum. It all sounds very good, very fashionable, very New Labour, but what does it actually mean?

What indeed is citizenship education? We are told that it means teaching children about their rights and responsibilities in a modern society, which presumably no one could object to.

In fact, it is highly objectionable. It means a particular conception of rights and responsibilities; one which does not favour our traditional British sense of freedom or of history, or of traditional morality ...

... citizenship education is nothing less than a means of getting young people into a state of mind where they are hungry for continuous political and social change, and perhaps eventually for the ultimate change: acceptance of a federal Europe ...

One can see why a government of lawyers, modernisers and professional politicians might like the idea of citizenship education. It is a way of making the next generation the same type of people as they are. But for the rest of us, that is a reason for resisting the very idea. (O'Hear 1999)

Education is, however, through and through a value-laden enterprise. Value issues and value choices cannot be eliminated and it is better not to evade them – for example, by pretending that they do not exist. What is important, therefore, is to recognize this reality and try to equip those involved in education to properly understand the complexity of the task they are engaged in – not only in these contested areas of personal, moral, social, spiritual and political education, but also in relation to the apparently more 'everyday' issues of subject teaching, assessment, the ways in which language is used in the classroom, relating to parents and their concerns, etc. All these aspects of education raise some issues which are indeed of a mainly technical or practical character; but underlying even the most mundane issues, value issues and questions of value priorities lurk.

What this book seeks to do is to link issues of 'theory' to these highly practical questions and dilemmas which teachers face every day of their lives. The contributors, in addition to being specialists in their various academic fields, are also, in almost every case, qualified teachers who have direct experience of working regularly with trainees, and alongside mentors and other staff in a wide range of schools which are part of the Cambridge PGCE partnership. The 'tone' of different articles varies. In some cases, particularly where the issues under discussion have a directly practical and 'chalk-face' relevance, authors address the reader in a direct and personal way. For example, Michael Reiss, discussing problems of selecting materials for sex education lessons, writes:

> If you do use published materials to help teach sex education in a secondary school, the most useful 'tip' is probably to get your pupils to critique the materials by discussing among themselves and with you – posing such questions as:
> * What useful things do these materials contain?
> * What angle do the authors seem to be taking?
> * Are there any ways the material could be better?

On other topics, particularly those which deal with broader issues of educational policy or primarily with conceptual issues, the tone is more 'academic'. Nevertheless, in all cases, all of us who have contributed to this book have tried to write in a way which is clear and accessible but without over-simplifying the complexity of the issues or the value problems they pose.

The layout of the book is self-explanatory. Part I deals with certain 'macro' issues: secondary schooling and its recent history, the school curriculum as a whole, and 'MARRA' (monitoring, assessment, recording, reporting and accountability); also discussed are two key aspects of classroom teaching and learning – teaching and learning *styles,* and the use of language in classrooms and across the curriculum. Part II focuses upon the school as a caring community and issues of educational opportunity – within the broader context of locality and environmental concerns. The topics included are pastoral care, children with special educational needs, equal opportunities in relation to gender, 'race' and class, the school and the community, and finally and most inclusively, environmental education. The third and final section is centred on subjects in which questions of values and controversiality are particularly prominent. The topics discussed are: values and controversial issues, moral education, citizenship and citizenship education, sex education, and education about drugs and substance abuse. In all the areas, the writers have taken account of recent research, the latest available policy initiatives and directives, and the likely shape of future programmes of initial teacher training, professional induction and Continuing Professional Development priorities.

JOHN BECK AND MARY EARL

Part I

Schooling, Curricula, Assessment, Teaching and Learning

Chapter 1

The Secondary School

PHILIP GARDNER

INTRODUCTION

What shapes the sequence of daily events that go on in any of the 5,000 or so secondary schools dotted all over England and Wales?

One obvious answer would be that the character of such events flows from the people who spend their everyday lives in the schools – the teachers and the pupils. Another answer might be to examine the influence of those with an immediate or direct interest in the life of a school – parents, governors, neighbouring businesses and the local community in general. Yet another would be to concentrate on those responsible for funding, administering and regulating the work of schools – central and local government, charities and the Churches.

In one way or another each of these groups exerts important effects upon the secondary school. Often, these effects may be short-lived; they make up the ceaseless daily round of the here and now and may fade and be soon forgotten. Sometimes, however, actions may have a deeper or more enduring significance. When this happens, their consequences become sedimented into patterns of routine practice over a long period. In other words, the consequences of some actions have an impact which extends well beyond their own time. What is done today may continue to shape the life of the secondary school many years hence.

This means that those who work in the secondary schools of the future will fully understand their professional and academic lives only to the degree that they understand something of decisions that were taken years before. The same applies to us. To understand the nature of the institutions within which we work, we have to know something of how they came to be as they are. In other words, we have to know something of our educational history (DfEE 1997, p. 10).

Some events in the evolution of the secondary school have had a particularly extensive force. In the nature of things, such events tend to take the form

of legislative action or executive decisions implemented by central government. Major pieces of educational legislation can exert a pervasive influence
over an entire educational generation and might even be seen as emblematic
of the dominating educational interests and priorities of a particular historical
period. We might take three such legislative turning-points as critical markers
in the historical development of the modern secondary school; they are the
Education Acts of 1988, 1944 and 1902.

Before we do this, however, it is important to remember that despite the
many changes which have marked the development of the secondary school
over the years, there is much that remains stubbornly familiar about patterns
of daily life in schools. This is because of the powerful institutional and situa-
tional constraints which schools themselves, at least in the form we have
known them throughout the whole of the twentieth century, exert upon
teachers and pupils. Such constraints mean that some things are extraordinar-
ily hard to change, and that many of the sights and sounds of the modern
secondary school – classrooms with the teacher standing at the front; crowded,
noisy corridors; regular assemblies; periodic bells; piles of books and paper-
work – would all be quite intelligible to the schoolgirl and schoolboy
memories of our grandparents.

We should also recognize that beneath the apparently clear-cut nomencla-
ture of 'secondary' schooling there lies a multitude of different institutional
forms, each with a distinctive and often complex history. We might, for
example, trace the historical development of single-sex schools, co-educational schools, voluntary schools associated with religious denominations,
comprehensive schools, grammar schools, city technology colleges, grant-
maintained schools, special schools, technical schools, secondary modern
schools, middle schools, private schools (including the confusingly named
'public' schools), residential schools, experimental schools, and, most recently,
beacon schools.

The educational patchwork which is represented by such a diverse list of
types of school could be simplified by dividing them into two broad groups –
the private and the public. At the beginning of the twentieth century, the
former was much larger than the latter; at the close of the century, the position
is reversed. The twentieth century, in other words, has seen the progressive
reformation of secondary schooling by successive governments as a principally public service. In consequence, it is with publicly-provided schools –
attended by more than 90 per cent of the nation's young people – that our
discussion is chiefly concerned.

The current Labour government envisages three basic categories of
publicly funded schools for the future. These will be:

- *community schools* (schools maintained by the local education authority
  (LEA) which also employs their staff and owns their premises);
- *aided schools* (religious schools employing their own staff, owning their
  own premises and contributing at least 15 per cent towards their own
  capital spending);

• *foundation schools* (schools, including former grant-maintained schools, employing their own staff and owning their own premises, but with their capital costs met wholly from public funds).

THE 1988 EDUCATION ACT AND AFTER

The Education Reform Act of 1988 has shaped – and will continue to shape – the educational generations of the late twentieth and early twenty-first centuries. Like all seminal pieces of legislation, the importance of the Act lay not just in its substantive provisions but in the degree to which its underlying principles reflected the state of wider social attitudes and aspirations. For example, a belief in the values of the market, together with an emphasis on deregulation, public accountability and the paramount interests of the consumer can all be seen as having a significant influence upon the construction of the Act. Such views were often expressed in the general perception that schools had to be opened up to new and broader influences and shaken out of the grip of a teaching profession that was characterized as looking inward to its own interests, and backwards to allegedly ineffective and unchallenging traditions of professional practice. This approach saw education as having been in some sense captured by its 'producers' – that is, the teachers – who had ultimately failed to respond to the interests of educational consumers, whether conceived as school students, parents or the nation as a whole. In order to address this concern, the 1988 Act invoked revolutionary new provisions in which novel institutional freedoms were combined with unprecedented control from the centre.

The first great achievement of the 1988 Act was to penetrate the traditional heart of the secondary teacher's professional autonomy through its specification of a national curriculum and associated attainment targets. Second, the Act endeavoured to give more freedom to the governors and headteachers of individual schools, particularly in terms of the disposition of devolved school finances and opportunities for seeking grant-maintained status outside the ambit of the LEA. In doing so, it marked an important moment in the shift of the balance of power in education away from the local education authorities. Third, the Act sought to make parental choices in the selection of a school, and parental voices in the day-to-day running of that school, more prominent. Fourth, it endeavoured to make that which went on in schools more visible to the world outside the school gates. As a consequence, public accountability has become a paramount concern. Among other things, this has led to the publication of examination results and other information in the form of school league tables, and to the establishment in 1992 of more formalized and judgemental procedures for the regular inspection of every school by the Office for Standards in Education (Ofsted) along with sweeping new powers to deal with schools perceived to be failing.

In the years since the passing of the Act, there have been some important modifications to this immensely ambitious programme. Most notably, as a result of the recommendations of the Dearing Report of 1993, the size of the statutory National Curriculum has been considerably slimmed. However, the cardinal principle that it is the legitimate business of the elected government to control the commanding heights of the curriculum is now an established one, and periodic curricular innovations from the centre – most recently the proposal to add courses in citizenship to the National Curriculum – can continue to be anticipated by the teachers of the twenty-first century. More generally, it would be fair to say that the broad policy direction established by the Act in other areas of secondary school life has been maintained and often augmented by successive governments since its passing. The Act has created a new landscape for secondary schools in which terms such as 'excellence', 'standards', 'partnership', 'leadership', 'performance', 'effectiveness' 'account-ability' and 'modernization' have become towering features. Under the influence of such concepts, many secondary schools have begun to re-think the nature of their educational mission, as well as the quality of their relationship with their local communities and the extent of their accountability to the many parties with a legitimate interest in the outcomes of what they do. Where these pervasive shifts will lead in terms of the future shape of the education system is uncertain, but the appetite for modernization is clearly not restricted to central government alone. Whilst many secondary teachers might originally have regarded the passing of the 1988 Act with some trepidation, ten years on the continuing, unrelenting accent upon change – some of it, until recently, unthinkable – has for others evinced a more receptive and optimistic mood.

One of the most important trends to emerge in this changed educational landscape has been a heightened emphasis upon diversity or flexibility in the provision of secondary education. Diversity, however, is an immensely prob-lematical concept when applied to an educational system which has historically been marked by a high degree of segmentation and unequal pro-vision. For those with memories reaching back to the mid-twentieth century, such an emphasis may raise images of an earlier period in which diversity in education could be seen as little more than a euphemism for profound struc-tural inequalities in the provision of secondary schooling. Politicians are well aware of the strength of such historical associations and the current Labour administration has sought to distance its support for diversity from any asso-ciation of this kind. The words of its 1997 White Paper, *Excellence in Schools* are instructive in this respect and offer an implicit critique of the inequalities of the pre-1988 period:

> We are not going back to the days of the 11-plus; but neither are we prepared to stand still and defend the failings of across-the-board mixed ability teaching . . . We intend to modernise comprehensive edu-cation to create inclusive schooling which provides a broad, flexible and motivating education that recognises the different talents of all children and delivers excellence for everyone. (DfEE 1997, p. 38)

In other words, from the perspective of the present government, diversity and flexibility are seen as strategies commensurate with both equality of opportunity and economic effectiveness. They are not seen to threaten that principle of parity of esteem between different forms of educational provision which underpinned much of the educational debate of the immediate post-war decades. Rather, the product of strategies of diversity and flexibility is presented in terms of finding more effective and appropriate ways of safe-guarding a wide range of learning outcomes across different groups of students. The related notion that such techniques might be identified, formalized and generalized across the teaching profession has important consequences for pedagogy. Just as the National Curriculum has codified that which is to be taught, pedagogical styles and practices are now seen by many as amenable to a similar degree of formalization and standardization. In this view, effective teaching practices may be identified through focused research and disseminated within the teaching profession as commended practical pedagogies, alongside associated organizational innovations such as 'target-grouping', 'fast-tracking' and 'accelerated learning' (DfEE 1997, p. 39).

The celebration of diversity and flexibility finds expression in other ways too. There is a new emphasis upon written agreements or contracts between home and school, together with innovative programmes of learning activities out of school hours, work-related learning, and information and communications technology.

All of these changes have been seen to call forth a new type of teaching force and this has led to further reforms centred upon the reshaping of pro-grammes of teacher training as a more school-based activity; the inception of specialist training for prospective headteachers and co-ordinators of special educational needs provision; the creation of a new grade of Advanced Skills Teacher; the proposed reformation of career structures for classroom teachers; and the recent inauguration of Educational Action Zones consti-tuted by small groups or 'families' of local secondary schools, working together with feeder primaries, local parents, business interests and local edu-cation authorities (DfEE 1997, pp. 39–41).

A further part of the move towards diversity and away from a single model of schooling – an idea which, in the recent past, was exemplified in the com-prehensive school movement of the 1960s and 1970s – has been the encouragement given to individual schools to play to their perceived strengths and to develop their own distinctive educational identities. Those that are judged to be most successful in this respect are to be named 'beacon' schools, acting as exemplars of good practice from whom it is anticipated that other schools should learn and might seek to emulate. In July 1998, 75 beacon schools were nominated by the Department for Education and Employment and will receive additional funding in return for sharing 'the secrets of their success' and thereby helping 'to raise standards in other schools, particularly in inner city areas'. From September 1999, a further 125 such schools were to be designated (DfEE 1998).

THE 1944 EDUCATION ACT AND AFTER

The 1944 Act – unlike its successor of 1988 – was forged in a period of strong national consensus and laid the foundation for the complex post-war settlement in secondary education. This period was principally dominated by the problem, not of nuancing the character of secondary education or ensuring its effectiveness, but of achieving an equitable experience of secondary schooling for all children – and not just a privileged minority – as a basic social principle. The 1944 Education Act was the culmination of the appeal, led by the radical writer R. H. Tawney, for – to use his great slogan – 'secondary education for all' which had begun to gather momentum from the 1920s.

The 1944 Act sought to end a great structural divide in educational provision which had its roots in the nineteenth century. This divide, echoing the sharp class divisions of British society, meant that much of the schooling provided in the interwar period continued to take place in hierarchically separated settings. Broadly, this meant that the majority of secondary school places available were filled by middle-class children, with most working-class children restricted to separate elementary schools throughout their entire school lives. The 1944 Act sought to end this segregation between the elementary and secondary sectors. It provided that elementary (now renamed primary) schooling and secondary schooling should be fused as a sequential unity of experience for all children. For the first time, every child in the nation was entitled to a secondary education as a right. In a post-war atmosphere marked by a sense of the collective sacrifice of a democratic citizenry in a just war, such a settlement was widely welcomed. But the sense of social justice and equality of opportunity in education went beyond the provision of secondary school places for all. The 1944 Act also abolished the right of publicly provided secondary schools to charge some of their pupils fees. This closed the pre-war loophole whereby wealthier parents had been able to buy places at local grammar schools for sons or daughters who had failed the competitive entry examination. The provisions of the Act meant not only that secondary schooling was now free to all, but that the allocation of a school place rested upon demonstrated individual merit and not on the ability to pay.

For two decades, the 1944 settlement enjoyed a honeymoon period – what historians have referred to as the 'period of consensus'. But it was not long before problems were looming. Free and universal secondary schooling was now a reality, but the new question was: what sort of secondary schooling, and for whom? Post-war thinking did not favour the notion of a common secondary school in which all children, regardless of ability or social background, might mix and share the same range of educational opportunities. This was because educational opinion was dominated by the view – inherited from the interwar years – that children's intellectual ability and academic potential was substantially innate. This assumption of fixed intelligence led many to the related position that children could be categorized at a relatively early age into scientifically identifiable types based upon distinctive educational aptitudes. On this view, the creation of common secondary schools was seen not merely as a futile exercise but a potentially damaging one in which innate ability and educational provision would be mis-matched.

A more appropriate solution was seen to be the establishment of differentiated and institutionally separate forms of school to cater for 'different' categories of ability and aptitude. After 1944, most local authorities set up systems of secondary schooling designed to cater for three categories of student which were popularly understood as the 'bookish', the 'handy' and the 'average'. In most localities it was assumed that this categorization could be effectively achieved through competitive examination for primary school pupils at the age of 11-plus. Upon the results of such examinations, pupils were allocated to the type of school which was deemed to be most appropriate to their demonstrated aptitude. The acceptance of this three-way division led to a post-war structure of schooling which became widely known as the tripartite system. The corresponding grades of school for each of the three groups were grammar schools, offering an academically based education leading on to university and the professions; technical schools, providing an education which prepared students for skilled manual and technical occupations; and secondary modern schools, offering a basic all-round education which was seen as sufficient for the needs of the generality of the nation's future workforce. As such, the courses of study offered by the secondary modern schools – in which the majority of the school population in the immediate post-war decades came to be educated – were not designed to lead to any form of external qualification. By contrast, grammar school courses culminated in the award of high status GCE (General Certificate of Education) certificates at Ordinary and Advanced level. It was not until 1965 that the less prestigious CSE (Certificate of Secondary Education) was inaugurated as an appropriate qualification for secondary modern students.

The distinction between the GCE and the CSE was symbolic of the most intractable problem which weighed on the post-war tripartite system. Despite the insistence by local and national politicians that each type of school should enjoy 'parity of esteem', this was never achieved. The dispersal of the nation's children into three effectively stratified levels of secondary schooling seemed to many to look back to the old hierarchical social inequalities of the interwar years and not forward to a more just post-war society. Instead of each level of schooling achieving a common respect, the technical and secondary modern schools were overshadowed by the perceived superiority of the grammar schools and the celebration of the academic curriculum they followed.

By the 1960s, the failure to achieve parity of esteem had massively undermined the tripartite system. Moreover, it was increasingly questioned whether children's educational ability could be definitively measured at the relatively early age of 11. Many frustrated parents came to believe that their children had been wrongly allocated to a form of schooling which was restricting their potential and from which there was no easy escape. There was a growing recognition that success in the 11-plus examination was not, as had been once thought, a simple, meritocratic reflection of innate ability but the product of a complex cocktail of factors in which home background, social class, gender and ethnicity all played their part, alongside individual aptitude. As a result, a new language of deprivation began to give voice to these concerns. This was a discourse which seemed to indicate that there was a social as well as an educational role for the secondary school. In this view, segregation by type of school could be seen as not only educationally invalid but also as damaging to the fabric of a democratic society itself. A form of common schooling increasingly commended itself for its potential to ensure the mixing of diverse social classes and ethnic groupings as well as for its promise to secure greater educational opportunity for individual students.

For many – and by no means only those on the political left – the answer to all these concerns lay in the spread of the comprehensive school movement. As a result, national reorganization along comprehensive lines moved to the top of the political agenda, and in 1965 the then Labour government issued the landmark Circular 10/65, inviting LEAs to draw up plans for comprehensive reorganization with the ultimate long-term goal of achieving '... the complete elimination of selection and separatism in secondary education ...' (Gordon *et al*. 1991, p. 190).

By the mid-1980s, the vast majority of pupils in the state sector were being educated in undifferentiated comprehensive schools. In the reorganization process, most secondary modern schools and, more controversially, very many traditional selective grammar schools disappeared in programmes of local amalgamation and reformation.

In 1970, Brian Simon and Caroline Benn had published an optimistic account of the progress to date of the comprehensive movement under the celebratory title *Halfway There*. The 'there' to which Simon and Benn looked forward has not turned out quite as they hoped or expected. In itself, this constitutes an important historical lesson. As Simon himself has pointed out on many occasions, all legislative and administrative interventions have unanticipated consequences, and in this respect educational policy has proved no exception to the rule. The comprehensive school is still with us in great numbers, as are its many supporters, but neither its practical nor its moral hegemony carry quite the same assurance as they once did.

THE 1902 EDUCATION ACT AND AFTER

The 1902 Act restructured the administration of education at the local level through the establishment of local education authorities which were required to take over responsibility for all levels of public educational provision in a locality. Before this point, the school boards – the Victorian forerunners of the LEAs – had had control only over the elementary sector of schooling. The widened role of the new LEAs marked an important stage in the complex and often combative history of relationship between local initiative and central prescription in the provision of public education which, like the even longer-running educational struggle between the Churches and the state, has been played out over the course of the twentieth century.

Under their new powers, many LEAs set about establishing their own secondary schools – the first publicly funded schools of this type. In most respects, the new LEA secondary schools modelled themselves on the older elite private sector secondary schools with all the appurtenances associated with such institutions – house systems, elaborate uniforms, team sports, honours boards, prefects, and so on. One important difference though was that, chiefly as a result of cost pressures, many of the new schools tended to be co-educational in place of the established tradition of single-sex schooling.

In terms of their curriculum, the new schools were required by central government to offer a course of study which, as has often been pointed out, was strikingly similar to that outlined in the National Curriculum specification of 1988, with the earlier formulation stipulating English, Mathematics, Science, Foreign Languages, Geography, History, Drawing, Physical Exercise and Manual Work or Housewifery (Aldrich 1996).

Another very important feature of these new maintained secondary schools was that, though they charged fees for most of their intake, a proportion of free places were set aside for able pupils from the public elementary school sector to begin their climb up the educational ladder. These scholarship places were to be awarded on the basis of competitive examination, usually at 11 plus. Those who were not able to set foot on the ladder – often as a consequence of their poverty rather than their lack of ability – were destined to remain in their lowly elementary schools until the statutory school leaving age of 14. (The minimum school-leaving age was raised to 15 in 1947 and 16 in 1972, where it currently remains.) The explicitly hierarchical and segmented character of the national educational system as it had evolved in the nineteenth century was therefore not fundamentally confronted. By the end of the First World War in 1918, however, the assumptions underlying that older system were increasingly challenged, both on the moral grounds of social justice and on the instrumental grounds of the massive national wastage of human capital represented by unequal access to educational opportunities. Four years later, Tawney's *Secondary Education for All* (1922) gave voice to these concerns and signalled the future direction of the development of secondary schooling.

How might we conclude this brief survey of the evolution of the secondary school in the twentieth century? In the first place we should note that secondary schooling is no longer the privilege of a select and wealthy few as it was at the beginning of the century. In the second, we should record that issues involving the principle of a common as against a differentiated experience of secondary schooling have been at the centre of educational debate for most of this period. Third, we should recognize that, from the earliest years of the century, there has been a persistent tension between, on the one hand, demands for educational equality of opportunity in secondary schooling and, on the other, the emphasis on the efficient use of the nation's human capital. Fourth, we should remind ourselves that, as for example in the case of the curriculum, continuity as well as change remains an important explanatory concept in understanding our educational history. Finally, we should note that the pervasive notion of differentiation in our national education system – now often expressed in the less controversial language of 'flexibility' – remains as central a policy issue at the close of the twentieth century as it was at its opening. The degree to which this principle can be seen to express itself within a context of genuine equality of opportunity rather than deep structural or institutional inequalities will be one of the major educational stories of the next century.

Chapter 2

The School Curriculum and the National Curriculum

JOHN BECK

INTRODUCTION

This chapter begins by talking very generally about the curriculum – considering the notion of curriculum in terms of its meaning as well as in terms of its scope, content and structure. There then follows a brief discussion of the important issue of the *control* of curricula, with particular reference to the various interest groups within society which seek to influence what children learn and how they learn it. The focus then becomes more specific, moving to an analysis of the emergence of a National Curriculum in England and Wales in 1988 and an examination of the various 'ideologies' which helped to shape it. The fourth section discusses how that National Curriculum has subsequently developed, with particular reference to the Revised National Curriculum introduced in 1995 as well as subsequent further revisions. Finally, the impact on the curriculum of various 'modernizing' tendencies is discussed, notably developments relating to the effects of wider economic change within an increasingly 'globalized' world.

WHAT IS MEANT BY 'CURRICULUM'?

In thinking about the school curriculum it is convenient initially to distinguish the following three issues:

1. The scope of 'curriculum'

Several writers on the curriculum have made a distinction between the formal (or planned) curriculum and the 'hidden' curriculum. The latter term has been used to refer to a wide range of aspects of school life associated with *how* schools transmit the knowledge which is part of the formal curriculum: for example, systems of rewards and punishments, the balance between mixed-ability grouping and setting, aspects of the school's pastoral system – all conveying messages about what the school really values and does not value (see, for example, Hargreaves 1982). In what follows, the emphasis will be on the *formal* curriculum. But in looking at any individual school, it is important to be alert to the nature of the relationship between the formal and hidden curriculum. Do similar principles underlie both or are there discrepancies? Are hidden messages being transmitted which may contradict the intended messages of the formal curriculum?

2. The content of the curriculum

In terms of its contents, any curriculum is a *selection* from all the worthwhile knowledge which schooling could potentially transmit. This implies that questions about *priorities* are inseparable from curriculum planning. An important issue, therefore, is to identify the *principles* that have been salient in shaping any particular curriculum. Three such principles which have often been important are: economic relevance, vocational relevance, and a conception of liberal education emphasizing the value of knowledge and understanding for its own sake.

A further basic question is whether the contents of the curriculum should be similar for all pupils or whether curricular provision should differ according to factors such as differences in individual ability, gender, social background, locality, etc. In nineteenth-century Britain, most working-class children received a form of education which was, with good reason, described as 'elementary'. Their more privileged counterparts typically received a version of liberal education. The National Curriculum, on the other hand, is based upon a principle that all pupils should, as far as possible, enjoy a common curriculum entitlement.

3. The structure of the curriculum

Curriculum structure has to do, at a fairly abstract level, with the nature of the elements that make up the curriculum, and their relationship to one another. Within the National Curriculum, the 'elements' are a set of discrete subjects, each separately timetabled and delivered by subject-specialist teachers. However, in the 1970s many innovative comprehensive schools organized their curricula within broad Faculty structures – for example, Integrated Humanities. They also planned the content within each of these areas as a series of thematic, inter-disciplinary topics; for example, 'war', 'the developing world', 'the family', etc. Radical *child-centred* approaches to education typically involve structures that are even more flexible – for example, where individual pupil choice strongly influences what shall be learned next, how much time shall be devoted to it, etc. Here, the 'elements' of the curriculum may be pupil-chosen topics which are different for different groups of pupils.

All forms of curriculum structure contain *some* set of rules or principles which shape the selection and sequencing of knowledge and the pacing of learning.

For this reason, it is not sensible to draw too sharp a distinction between curriculum structure and curriculum content. Often, common principles shape both together.

THE CONTROL OF THE CURRICULUM

Because what children learn in school powerfully influences the thinking, attitudes and beliefs of future citizens, the content of the curriculum is normally, to a greater or lesser extent, contested. In certain totalitarian regimes, the use of the education system to inculcate some version of a dominant ideology can be particularly blatant. However, in contemporary democratic societies – which tend to be pluralistic both politically and culturally – a range of 'key players' compete (and sometimes co-operate) to influence what is institutionalized as 'educational knowledge'. Among the most important of these 'players' are politicians and political parties, state bureaucrats, religious organizations, employers' organizations and trade unions, sections of the communications media, and last but by no means least, teachers and the various organizations which represent them (teacher unions, subject associations, educational 'theorists' in higher education, etc.). All these groups and sub-groups have specific vested interests which they seek to defend or promote. Very often, members of such interest groups tend to see a natural coincidence between their own sectional concerns and what they take to be the interests of society as a whole. This being so, there is often good reason to be sceptical of the claims of those who engage in 'needs talk' – i.e. those who confidently tell us that 'society *needs* "x", or "y", or "z"'.

THE INTRODUCTION OF A NATIONAL CURRICULUM IN ENGLAND AND WALES: RATIONALES

As the previous section suggests, at any point in time, the content and structure of school curricula tends to reflect the relative power and influence of diverse interest groups. The recent history of how a National Curriculum came to be introduced in England and Wales in 1988 clearly illustrates the operation of these processes of curriculum contestation. The *idea* of a national curriculum drew support from various sources, and it important to appreciate that, even among its supporters, there was by no means a consensus about *what kind* of national curriculum was desirable.

Curriculum entitlement

One influential set of voices was those who believed that the introduction of a national system of comprehensive schooling in the 1960s and 1970s had been an important organizational reform but that it needed to be complemented by an equally radical revision of the *content* of education. The establishment of a national system of 'common' secondary schools, it was argued, implied that such schools should provide broadly similar curricular experiences for all their pupils. One set of considerations here related to equality of educational opportunity. All pupils in such schools, it was proposed, should be regarded as having a common curriculum *entitlement*. Now this clearly is an important argument – but it is also incomplete. There are certain fundamental questions which the notion of entitlement does not in itself address. Most importantly, it provides no answers to the questions: 'Entitlement to what?' – and 'Why?'

Liberal education for all: promoting rational autonomy

One set of answers to these questions was provided by the work of certain liberal philosophers of education, many of whom were associated with the University of London Institute of Education in the 1960s and 1970s (see, for example, Hirst and Peters 1970, Bailey 1984). These writers argued that pupils of all abilities – and not just an academic minority – should be offered a broad liberal education. A key aim of this particular kind of liberal education is the development of *rational autonomy*. All pupils should receive an education designed to help them to become more capable of making their own reasoned decisions about what might, for them, constitute 'the good life'. Liberal education should aim to free young people from 'the present and the particular' – i.e. from the narrow perspectives and preconceptions of whatever sub-section of society they were brought up in. Liberal education would do this by developing in young people both a respect for reasoning and evidence, and a capacity to employ rational thought and argument to interrogate the world around them. The disposition to ask: 'What's the evidence for that?', to seek reasoned justifications, and so on, is therefore central to this particular conception of liberal education.

Such reasoning, however, cannot take place in a vacuum. To think seriously about such matters requires that young people acquire the relevant kinds of knowledge and understanding. Exactly what forms of knowledge and understanding should have highest priority within this kind of liberal education has been (and continues to be) the subject of some debate. But there is broad agreement that it is desirable that young people should understand the physical, non-human world (through mathematics and the natural sciences) and also the human world of society and culture – including their own place within it. *Moral* reasoning and understanding are also seen as central – not least because thinking seriously about what one ought and ought not to do, and why, is an essential element of moral agency and autonomy.

According to the philosophers of the 'London School' therefore, children and young people should be offered a curriculum which is broad and balanced in the sense that it includes humanistic, aesthetic, social, political and moral education as important elements, in addition to mathematics, science and technology. What was most genuinely radical about this approach to liberal education was the contention that it should be offered to *all* the nation's children. Previously, it was widely accepted that only an academic minority (such as those who went to grammar and independent schools) could cope with a curriculum of this kind, and that it was better to provide 'less able' pupils with something less demanding and/or more vocationally relevant.

Neo-conservative versions of liberal education

During the educational debates which surrounded the introduction of the National Curriculum, however, other voices and interest groups were arguing for a rather different kind of liberal education. They too wanted to provide all children with a broad curriculum whose purposes were not primarily economic or vocational, but their basic agenda was one of *cultural restoration.* They advocated a return to 'tradition'; they wanted to use the curriculum to help to reinstate orthodox Christian belief, respect for traditional values and institutions, and a stronger emphasis on Britain's cultural heritage. Writers of this 'neo-conservative' persuasion contributed to a series of polemical 'Black Papers on Education' between 1969 and 1977 (see Cox and Dyson 1969). These publications deplored what they depicted as a decline in standards in grammar, literacy and numeracy, and the harm allegedly done by the intro-duction of comprehensive schooling. A similar critique – of the allegedly malign influence of multiculturalism, anti-racism, anti-sexism, and moral per-missiveness – was put forward by members of the neo-conservative Hillgate Group in the mid-1980s immediately prior to the introduction of the National Curriculum (see, for example, Scruton 1987). The characteristically baleful tone of such writers is caught in the following quotation from Dr Edward Norman, then Dean of Peterhouse College, Cambridge: 'the values of this country are under threat; society discloses advanced symptoms of moral collapse . . . a great moral chaos will accumulate within a few decades if the whole absurdity is allowed to go on that long' (Norman 1977, p. 103). These lobbyists supported the introduction of a national curriculum composed of 'tried and tested' traditional subjects, with an emphasis on the cultural heritage of 'the British people'. They were not unsuccessful. The inclusion of RE as a Basic Subject, with at least 50 per cent of the available time devoted to Christianity, a stronger emphasis on British art and literature, more space given to British history, etc. are among their achievements. In all these respects, therefore, neo-conservatives were influential in establishing a version of a national curriculum which was academic rather than vocational, and broad and reasonably balanced in its composition. In these senses, the National Curriculum introduced by the 1988 Education Reform Act was, broadly, a liberal curriculum.

However, it is important to highlight a key difference between the under-lying educational aims of neo-conservatives, on the one hand, and those of liberal philosophers like Peters or Bailey, on the other. Whilst the latter are committed to intellectual *openness* – to widening pupils' intellectual horizons so that they may become more rationally autonomous – the former are, at least to some extent, concerned to promote a kind of *closure*: to socialize children into the acceptance of a set of specific and pre-selected beliefs and values, arguably constructed around a highly selective, conservative, and idealized version of the nation's past.

THE NATIONAL CURRICULUM: BALANCE, DEVELOPMENT AND CHANGE SINCE 1988

The distinction, present from the outset, between Core and Foundation subjects within the National Curriculum, itself represents a clear signalling of priorities. This is heavily reinforced by the system of national tests which has become an ever more prominent element of the total apparatus of curriculum prescription in England and Wales. The 'effectiveness' and performance of schools is increasingly judged by the achievements of their pupils in the three Core Subjects – achievements which are published both locally and nationally. For younger pupils, this stress on Core Subjects – and on Maths and English in particular – is understandable and to some extent justifiable. Aspects of these subjects (and increasingly of ICT too) are part of what Bailey calls 'the serving competences' – i.e. prerequisites for moving into the knowledge and under-standing of the rest of the curriculum. Beyond this, however, there is room for significantly more debate about what constitutes a desirable curriculum balance. Not a few writers have suggested that even in the original version of the National Curriculum, certain important areas of knowledge and experi-ence were under-represented: notably the ethical, the social and political, and the aesthetic. And there is little doubt that after 1988, the National Curriculum was subjected to a succession of changes, most of which tended to shift the balance even more in favour of those subjects which have, or are thought to have, importance for employment and for national economic success.

The Dearing Report of 1993, which led to the Revised National Curricu-lum introduced in 1995, drastically reduced the content of all the Foundation Subjects across Key Stages 1 to 3, whilst in some ways strengthening the sig-nificance of numeracy and literacy within Mathematics and English, and also introducing Information Technology as a new Foundation subject (Dearing 1993).

Moreover, as former Chief HMI Eric Bolton has claimed, it is arguable that beyond the age of 14, the effect of the Dearing reforms was that 'the National Curriculum was deconstructed' (Bolton 1994). Only English, Maths and a single science, plus 'elements' of a modern language and technology, remained statutory. In effect, Dearing allowed and even encouraged secondary schools to promote *specialization* after the age of 14, for example permitting schools to offer three separate science subjects for some of their most able pupils, while providing a range of pre-vocational options for the less academic. The original vision of a *common* curriculum extending from age 5 to age 16 was thus seriously compromised. Not, of course, that this vision had ever been uni-versally shared. Margaret Thatcher herself stated that her conception of what should be compulsory never extended beyond the Core subjects and RE. And others on the political right have been even more vigorous in their condemna-tion of centralized state prescription of what pupils should be taught. The

free-marketeer Sheila Lawlor, for example, has written: 'the National Curriculum has become the organ for enforcing an educational consensus on all
and crushing dissent by the weight of the law' (Lawlor 1994).

The New Labour government which came into office in 1997 continued
this restructuring process, further strengthening the emphasis on basic
numeracy and literacy at the expense of the Foundation subjects – at least
within primary education. In 1998, 'new arrangements for curriculum flexibility' were announced: these permitted primary schools to partially disregard
the Statutory Orders for six of the Foundation Subjects in order to make space
for the government's prioritizing of basic skills in the areas of literacy,
numeracy and ICT. This development did not, however, give primary schools
greater curricular autonomy since 'the literacy hour' and 'the numeracy hour'
involved a further increase in levels of centralized prescriptiveness – not only
in terms of content but also with regard to *methods* of teaching. New Labour's
plans for further National Curriculum revisions to be implemented from
September 2000 onwards were published in May 1999 in the form of a consultation document (QCA and DfEE 1999). No *basic* revision of the structure or
framework of the National Curriculum was contemplated: all of the Core and
Foundation subjects, as well as RE as a basic subject, were retained. However,
programmes of study were generally rewritten to be 'less prescriptive and
more flexible' (*ibid.*, p. 3); the statutory framework for ICT across the curriculum was strengthened; and a more explicit rationale for the National
Curriculum as a whole was provided. A significant new development,
however, was the addition of non-statutory guidance for personal, social and
health education (PSHE) across all four Key Stages, and the inclusion of a new
statutory 'foundation subject for citizenship' (*ibid.*, p. 28) at Key Stages 3 and
4 only. (These proposals are discussed more fully in the Introduction to this
volume, and in Chapter 13.)

TRADITIONALISTS AND MODERNIZERS IN THE WIDER CURRICULUM DEBATE

In the campaign leading up to the General Election of 1997, Tony Blair
famously declared that New Labour's greatest priority was 'education, education, education'. It is important to appreciate that this was more than political
rhetoric. New Labour's most influential strategists had become increasingly
convinced that certain features of global economic change made it imperative
to place education at the top of the government's policy agenda. This overall
analysis suggested that the world economic system, particularly in the era
since the fall of the USSR, had entered a qualitatively new phase. Allegedly
irreversible forces of globalization and accelerating technological change, as
well as the growing power of trans-national companies in channelling new
investment around the world, were all working together to create a scenario in
which the key determinant of national levels of employment was the educational quality of the workforce (Blair 1998). If Britain was to remain
competitive and able to attract inward investment, its young people needed to

be highly skilled in economically relevant respects, and the country needed to raise its lagging position in international league tables of literacy and numeracy. This analysis was part of a wider perspective on economic change which is sometimes termed 'Post-Fordist'. Briefly, this suggests that advanced economies are undergoing a shift from 'mass' and mainly industrial production, to the production of a much more diversified range of more specialized goods and *services*, in response to rapidly changing patterns of demand operating on a global scale. This, in turn, implies growing unpredictability in a variety of respects and it requires a response of 'flexible specialization' which makes quite new demands on employees at all levels of the workforce. In particular, the new productive technologies are seen as placing a premium on knowledge-based and information-processing skills as well as requiring a more generalized capacity to be flexible in terms of readiness to accept recurrent retraining in the face of a future which no one can predict. On this view, 'jobs for life' and a stable lifelong career within a single organization are things of the past.

The key implications for education are seen as focusing upon two main areas: first, questions about the content of an education congruent with these developments; and second, questions of broadening *access* to such a re-shaped education (because people at *all* levels of the workforce will need to improve their skills). The educational restructuring that is seen to be necessary goes much wider than the curriculum of schools. It needs, say its advocates, to involve radical changes to *higher* education – not least in terms of weakening the 'stranglehold' on innovation that has been for too long exerted by traditional forms of elite liberal education, whose bastions have been the highest-status 'old' universities (notably Oxbridge), as well as the independent schools. The most influential supporters of these changes have been some of the supporters of vocational education – notably those who have sought to link vocationalism to a range of 'progressive' innovations in terms of teaching and learning styles, and non-traditional modes of assessment. Key terms in the vocabulary of these 'curriculum modernizers' (as also in the vocabulary of the theorists of Post-Fordism) are 'empowerment' and 'ownership'. What is needed, it is argued, is to empower students by giving them more effective ownership of their own education and training. What this involves in practice are developments such as:

- modular course structures and extended student choice, which enable students themselves (rather than academic 'experts') to structure their own curriculum in ways that are personally relevant;
- a weakening of the boundaries between 'theory' and 'practice', so that a wide range of vocational activities can become part of higher education, and so that students can be assessed on the basis of their practical competence/performance as much as on their 'theoretical' knowledge as measured by traditional written examinations;
- greater vocational relevance of course content across a wider range of courses;

- 'education for capability' as much as for academic excellence;
- continuous assessment and credit accumulation rather than end-of-course examinations;
- 'portability' of qualifications between institutions, as one element in a policy of widening educational access;
- greater permeability of the boundary between school, and further and higher education;
- greater provision of part-time study and greater flexibility in opportunity to mix full-time and part-time study.

Many recent curriculum innovations in the 14–19 curriculum within schools clearly illustrate the impact of this kind of thinking. Examples include the huge growth in popularity of A-levels in subjects such as Business Studies, as well as the increase in the provision of GNVQ courses not only for less academic students in Years 11, 12 and 13, but also as increasingly popular alternatives to A-levels.

The watchwords of the modernizers' approach, then, include the following: choice, empowerment, flexibility, access, competence, skill, relevance. Interestingly, as numerous commentators have noted, this modernizing project of educational reform unites certain educationalists and politicians of the left with certain of those of the right – creating a powerful alliance. As the Robertson Report noted:

> the support of student choice and flexibility commands widespread support in principle. It conveniently unites the radicals of the Right (markets, freedom of choice) and of the Left (democratic participation, student empowerment) against the conservatives of the Right (elite participation and the preservation of standards) and of the Left (sovereignty of the academic, supremacy of the unified course, the student as apprentice). (HEQC 1994, p. 119, cited in Avis 1996, p. 114)

It is therefore unsurprising that a government pursuing a so-called Third Way in politics appears more than a little enamoured of these 'new directions'. Nevertheless, the tensions which are indicated in the passage just quoted remain significant and constitute a source of continuing vigorous debate.

Critics of these modernizing tendencies have expressed various kinds of reservations:

- Academic traditionalists claim that the result of such changes will be an inexorable 'dumbing down' which is said to be already pervasive in the USA, where it is seen as being reinforced by strongly relativist multicultural and post-modernist tendencies. In Britain, traditionalists like Melanie Phillips attacked Sir Ron Dearing's review of post-16 education (published in 1996) on the ground that it 'proposed the dilution of A-level with vocational elements and the gradual blurring of the differences between disparate qualifications to produce an illusion of equivalence'.

According to Phillips 'the national educational currency was being devalued' (Phillips 1996, p. 185). In the event, the government moved only a limited distance along this particular modernizing track – providing 'encouragement' to students and institutions to broaden the scope of A-levels but stopping well short of enforcing such diversification.

- Other critics fear that the rise of vocationalist tendencies will operate to cut students off from those elaborated forms of knowledge which provide the fundamental sources of criticism of the dominance of vocational and instrumental interests within education, replacing them with technicist forms of 'training' whose hidden curriculum is education for conformity and complacency. Some critics of 'competency-based' modes of teacher training have identified similar dangers in the removal of 'theory' from teacher training programmes (see Moore 1994).
- A third criticism is that the modernizers' emphasis on 'ownership' and 'empowerment' is little more than rhetoric. Such critics draw attention to the closely circumscribed limits of much of this 'empowerment', arguing that the real motor of these changes is the wish of employers to promote ever greater 'flexibilization' of the workforce. This, say the critics, may prove a more than mixed blessing, since it carries with it the potential for growing job insecurity, increased casualization, and a widening of pay differentials between the new meritocratic 'haves' and an increasingly numerous group of 'have nots'. Furthermore, the claim that such flexibilization is inevitable because of 'irreversible' globalization is a smoke-screen concealing the interests of those sectors of (mainly American) finance capital dedicated to promoting worldwide free trade and the spread of Western consumer culture. Such forces are more correctly seen as dangerously destructive both of local cultures and the global environment. The key priority should be to resist them (see Gray 1998).

Chapter 3

Monitoring, Assessment, Recording, Reporting and Accountability

JOHN RAFFAN AND KENNETH RUTHVEN

INTRODUCTION

Every area of education raises philosophical and practical issues, and probably none more so than assessment. We all know how it feels to be assessed, to have our work marked, to sit tests and examinations and to read reports on our attainments and progress. But do we agree that it was all 'fair'? Was it helpful to us and our teachers? As every teacher has a major professional role in assessment, we must appreciate and manage both its possibilities and limitations.

The title for this chapter is drawn from Section C of the document *Standards for the Award of Qualified Teacher Status* (DfEE 1998). Let us briefly examine each of the terms of the title in turn and relate them to successful practice as a teacher:

- 'Monitoring' means keeping in touch with your pupils' learning, the difficulties that they are experiencing and the progress that they are making. The term also summarizes the various procedures used by any organization responsible for education, from schools to local and national government, to check on standards and progress.
- 'Assessment' refers to any process which gives information about pupils' learning. Informal classroom processes include observing pupils tackling a task, questioning them about their work, looking at their written recording, or listening in on their discussions. More formal processes include testing and setting assignments for marking, and the national system of tests and examinations.
- 'Recording' means maintaining up-to-date records of the classroom experience and achievement of individual pupils, relating these systematically to the agreed curriculum and assessment framework laid down by the National Curriculum, or the corresponding requirements of upper secondary courses and qualifications.

- 'Reporting' means preparing a summary overview of the performance of individual pupils. Intended both for official purposes and to advise pupils and their parents, pupil reports must relate achievement to the standards defined by national frameworks for curriculum and assessment, and must convey this and broader information about the pupils' learning in a way which pupils and parents can understand.
- 'Accountability' refers to the important part that formal assessment plays in evaluating the performance not just of pupils but of their teachers and schools.

Through the processes of recording and reporting, teachers and schools demonstrate their seriousness of purpose – and their success – in promoting pupils' learning. The results of public examinations for schools are usually published in local newspapers and, more controversially, scores based on these results are calculated to provide national and local 'league tables'.

PURPOSES OF ASSESSMENT

Much of the debate about assessment, whether at national or at school level, is concerned with 'How?' questions, with techniques of testing and interpretation and the reporting of results. There is another debate, usually less public but hardly less important, about the 'Why?' questions, the nature of assessment and its purposes.

Analysis of thinking and performance

Assessment can give insights into very specific aspects of the thinking and performance of pupils. How are they thinking about a particular situation? Where and why is skilled performance on some task breaking down? Using assessment to ask and answer such questions improves the information available to the teacher and makes it possible to identify and address learning difficulties.

Feedback to pupils, teachers and parents

Feedback should be the most important use of assessment. The procedures may range from informal 'impressions' to formal written tests, but the main purpose is to keep pupils and teachers informed about progress and achievements during the course or in relation to a particular episode of teaching. This is known as *formative* assessment, as it guides the ongoing processes of teaching and learning and is integral to these processes. Formative assessment is in contrast to *summative* assessment which attempts to summarize and evaluate the outcomes of pupils' performance at the end of a course of study but is, partly for this very reason, unlikely to help change their performance.

Motivation

Most learners find that the feedback on their performance, gained from assessment, is positively motivating. The prospect of a test or examination also usually concentrates minds and acts as an incentive to both pupils and teachers; but using this external stimulus effect of assessment does raise the issue of how far it may become an instrument of coercion in work or behaviour. The inclusion of a wider range of evidence in documents such as a Record of Achievement can help to raise pupils' self-esteem and motivation.

Prediction and selection

Assessment of pupils' present attainments gives teachers evidence which they can use to attempt predictions about future performance and progress. When this is undertaken at the end of a course of study, typically in summative, end-of-year tests, the predictions often lead to selection. Within a school there is usually some form of assessment before pupils are assigned to 'ability groups' in sets, bands or streams. Selection is probably the major outcome of the public examinations system, as the results play an important part in recruitment to further and higher education and employment.

Monitoring and maintaining standards

Assessments may lead to the award of qualifications, such as public examination grades, university degrees or awards from professional bodies. These should provide reasonable guarantees that successful candidates have achieved acceptable standards; we are unlikely, for example, to have any confidence in the competence of an unqualified medical doctor or engineer. The demanding specifications in the standards for the award of Qualified Teacher Status are intended to improve both the professional capabilities and the status of teachers. Analysis of data gathered from National Curriculum tests allows national monitoring of standards of pupil performance at the different Key Stages.

Controlling the content of the curriculum and teaching styles

For many teachers, this is a somewhat undesirable side-effect, rather than a main purpose of assessment. There is no doubt, however, that the techniques and frequency of assessment and examinations do profoundly affect both the content of the curriculum and how it is taught. (This is discussed further in the later section on 'Impact'.)

FORMATIVE ASSESSMENT AND EFFECTIVE TEACHING

Research into the use of formative assessment in classroom settings has confirmed the important contribution that it can make to effective teaching and learning. Informal classroom assessment offers immediate information to support important teaching functions. It provides timely evidence to guide teachers' interventions in support of pupils' learning, and their management of the ongoing lesson. Formative assessment helps teachers to match the planning of future lessons more effectively to the learning characteristics and needs of particular groups of pupils. It also provides the basis from which teachers can give pupils constructive oral and written feedback, and help them set appropriate targets for the development of their work.

This body of research identified approaches to assessment which are particularly helpful and unhelpful. Black and Wiliam (1998) surveyed 600 research studies from across the world, conducted at levels from nursery school to university undergraduate, and in subjects from Mathematics to PE. These studies indicate that teacher assessment which diagnoses pupils' difficulties and provides constructive feedback leads to significant learning gains, particularly for lower-attaining pupils. The effect is to reduce the spread of attainment in a group while at the same time raising performance overall, so tackling what is often seen as an intractable – and inevitable – problem of a 'tail' of under-achievement and consequent pupil alienation. The most modest improvement found in these studies raised the performance of the average pupil to the level previously achieved by only one in three. In Britain, improvement on this scale would push GCSE performance up by between one and two grades per subject.

So what exactly are teachers doing in classrooms where formative assessment produces such remarkable effects? The survey identifies five factors seemingly crucial for successful learning, and a further five that hinder it.

Standards are raised by:

* regular classroom testing and the use of results to adjust teaching and learning rather than for competitive grading;
* enhanced feedback between teacher and pupils which may be oral or in the form of written comments on work or both;
* the active involvement of all pupils;
* careful attention to the motivation and self-esteem of pupils, encouraging them to believe that they can learn what is being taught;
* time allowed for *self*-assessment by pupils, discussion in groups and dialogue between teacher and pupils.

Standards are not raised by:

* tests which encourage rote and superficial learning, even when teachers claim they wish to develop understanding;
* failure by teachers to discuss and review testing methods between themselves;
* over-emphasis on the giving of marks and grades at the expense of useful advice to learners;
* approaches which compare pupils in a way which persuades them that the purpose is competition rather than personal improvement, and which demotivate some pupils;

* feedback, testing and record-keeping which serves a managerial rather than a learning function.

ISSUES OF VALIDITY, RELIABILITY, PRACTICABILITY AND IMPACT OF ASSESSMENT

Validity

Validity in assessment means that the procedures test what the assessors intend. This may seem self-evident, but achieving validity is often difficult. Among several types of validity, the variety which most concerns teachers as assessors is *content validity*. It requires that assessment procedures should be well matched to the actual content and objectives of the taught course, covering as much as possible of the syllabus and not going beyond it. Validity would be limited, for example, if an assessment system was established for a course of study with a substantial practical or oral content (e.g. in the sciences, languages or art) without giving the candidates opportunities to show their competences in practical or oral activities. If candidates for an examination are not familiar with particular styles of questions (e.g. multiple choice or essay writing), a paper containing these questions would lack validity.

Assessors try to ensure high content validity for any test or examination by arranging that the objectives and content of the taught course are sampled as fully as possible. It helps to draw up a specification grid; an example for an examination in Humanities is shown in Table 3.1.

Table 3.1: A specification grid

Objectives	%	Culture and beliefs 50%	Cooperation and conflict 25%	Resources and conservation 25%
Recall	30	10	10	10
Interpretation	30	20	5	5
Analysis	20	10	5	5
Application	10	5	2.5	2.5
Evaluation	10	5	2.5	2.5

The grid shows the skills and abilities (objectives) in the first column and, in the other column headings, the main content topics to be tested. Percentages of marks are allocated to each objective and content section; these are known as the 'weightings'. For example: the 'interpretation' of topics concerning 'Culture and Beliefs' has a 20 per cent weighting in the test. Public examination specifications (syllabuses) always publish the weightings for assessment objectives, skills and abilities to be examined, and much use is made of specification grids by examiners to ensure high validity.

Reliability

In general terms, reliability is about consistency and fairness of the assessment procedures. Reliability of test and examination scores possibly causes more concern at national level than any other aspect of assessment, as assessment systems rely upon an assumption that competent assessors would, in principle, all award the same mark to the same piece of work. In practice this is notoriously difficult to achieve and every year tales are told in the examining world, occasionally appearing all too publicly, about unfortunate inconsistencies in standards of marking. Reliability of marking can be affected by many personal factors; the assessor, whether a teacher with a set of test responses or an examiner with examination scripts, may not give each script the same amount of attention or they may be influenced by poor handwriting.

There is always a concern about how representative, how generalizable and how dependable is any result, as the pupils/candidates themselves, for personal reasons, may not have performed reliably at their normal standard at the time of the test.

Awarding Bodies (Examination Boards) are the guardians of reliability for national examinations and much of the fee income they receive is allocated to:

- co-ordination meetings where examiners approve a mark scheme for a paper and agree the standards of answers expected;
- moderation procedures where marks from different examiners are checked for consistency;
- possible multiple marking of the same scripts;
- statistical techniques for monitoring sources of unreliability in test papers and the treatment of results.

Practicability

All assessment incurs costs in time, effort and finance and, in the case of national tests and examinations, the costs of trying to ensure that they are valid and reliable can be very high. Anyone involved with assessment systems has to establish some form of time and financial controls.

Formative assessment has positive effects on learning, and teachers, in general, are willing to accept the time and effort involved in this kind of testing, marking and processing of results. Summative assessment, however, often raises more problems of practicability with obvious examples in the assessment of course work, oral proficiency in languages, and practical performance in the arts and sciences. To what extent might it be practicable and cost-effective to employ external examiners to ensure consistency in course-work assessment across a large number of examination centres? Would it be practicable to provide candidates with word processors in examinations, as many are able to use a keyboard quickly but cannot produce their best performance in handwriting?

Impact

Assessment has a profound effect upon teaching and learning. Indeed, as mentioned above, effective learning (and hence teaching) could hardly proceed without the feedback that assessment provides.

We must also recognize the impact of assessment where its procedures may actually control the teaching and learning and perhaps distort the original intentions of the designed course. The history of education is full of concerns about teachers 'teaching to the test'; most recently this has been raised in the case of the tests used to monitor standards achieved under the National Curriculum. Other national testing procedures have produced an examination-led curriculum in the later years of secondary education, with specifications (syllabuses) from the Awarding Bodies determining the content and, to some extent, even the style of teaching and learning.

It is an issue for debate in education as to whether this impact of assessment upon the curriculum is an unintended side-effect rather than deliberate policy. Indeed, educational policy-makers tend to make statements such as 'The assessment process itself should not determine what is to be taught and learned' (National Curriculum Task Group on Assessment and Testing 1987). Many practitioners and observers who experience the realities of the educational system will, however, recognize the pragmatic assertion of J. D. Rowntree (1977):

> If we wish to discover the truth about an educational system, we must look into its assessment procedures. What student qualities and achievements are actively valued and rewarded by the system? ... The spirit and style of student assessment defines the *de facto* curriculum.

Arguments can become quite lively over the impact and advantages and disadvantages of external and internal modes of assessment, and these are outlined in the following section.

ISSUES OF ASSESSMENT MODES

Comparisons of external and internal (teacher) assessment

External assessment occurs when an external organization, typically an Awarding Body (Examination Board), specifies all of the conditions of assessment, from the objectives and content to the setting of examination papers, and organizes the marking and processing of results.

Internal assessment (now more officially recognized as 'teacher assessment') is provided by teachers who organize the course of study and includes, for example, assessment of coursework essays, projects, practical and oral assignments. In the case of public examinations, internal (teacher) assessment is guided by specifications from the Awarding Bodies. Teachers are responsible for most of the setting of assessment tasks and marking the work produced; the Awarding Bodies provide a framework for approval of assessment procedures and moderation of the marks and of teachers' judgements.

Advantages of an external assessment mode

- It provides assessment procedures unaffected by personal relationships between teachers and pupils.
- It reduces the possibility of conflict for a teacher between their role as a teacher and as an assessor.
- It supports reliability of assessment by providing for uniformity of practice and standards, with all pupils being assessed upon common qualities by common criteria.
- It supports practicability of assessment by concentrating resources and expertise for setting and marking.
- It provides an independent assessment whose results are more likely to be accepted by the 'users' of examination results such as employers and admissions officers in universities.
- It enables the assessment procedures in, for example, practical activities to exert an influence on the nature of the work carried out in schools.

Disadvantages of an external assessment mode

These are largely in terms of *reducing the validity* of the assessment.

- Assessment techniques are limited to those which can be administered by an external agency such as an Awarding Body.
- The assessment is limited to the outcomes of work under examination conditions and does not include a consideration of the quality of performance as it happens.
- The number of occasions upon which the assessment can take place is limited by administrative considerations.
- The assessment may narrow the teaching objectives to those which can be assessed in an external mode; for example it may restrict the types of practical and other course work carried out in schools.

Advantages of an internal (teacher) assessment mode

These are largely in terms of *enhancement of the validity* of the assessment.

- It requires teachers to think about assessment in terms of the educational and assessment objectives of their courses.
- It makes possible the development of assessment procedures which are suited to the facilities available in particular schools and which are closely related to the courses devised by those schools.
- The dangers of untypical failure or success are reduced, by providing assessment possibilities on a number of occasions.

- It enables pupils to be assessed during their performance, for example while undertaking practical tasks, as well as upon the outcomes.

Disadvantages of an internal (teacher) assessment mode

- With many different teachers acting as assessors, reliability of assessment is more difficult to achieve and comparisons of standards between school and school are possibly less reliable.
- Teachers are often concerned about their role as assessor in relationships with pupils.
- It can place a severe strain upon teachers in terms of time, effort and expertise.
- It is likely to be more subjective, certainly less objective, than an external mode and the 'users' may be less confident about the validity and reliability of the results.

ISSUES OF COMPARISONS OF PERFORMANCE: CRITERION- AND NORM-REFERENCING

Many tests are designed to show whether or not a candidate has become sufficiently competent to perform at a predetermined and stated level. Familiar examples of these 'mastery' and 'can-do' tests include the driving test and graded examinations in music or languages. The tests have explicit criteria for success, and the individual candidate either satisfies the criteria or should undertake more practice and re-enter. This type of assessment is said to be *criterion-referenced.*

In criterion-referenced assessment there is no intention to compare the performance of individual candidates. This is in contrast to *norm-referenced* assessment procedures which are intended to be discriminating and to distinguish between higher and lower achievers in a group of individuals who have undertaken a course. For norm-referenced procedures a test would contain questions across a range of difficulty and the candidates' marks would be widely spread. The results should allow the assessors to compare the performances of candidates against each other and with the 'norm' for the class or age group.

Teachers have to interpret the marks and grades gained from assessment to pupils, parents, employers and admissions officers in further and higher education. It is essential that they distinguish between marks and grades achieved through criterion-referenced and norm-referenced assessments.

National Curriculum standardized assessment tests (familiarly called 'SATs') are criterion-referenced tests, as criteria are published in 'level descriptions' for performance at each attainment level. They are intended to help teachers to monitor their pupils' progress against national standards and to allow the government, through the Qualifications and Curriculum Authority (QCA), to undertake national monitoring of schools' performance.

Some years ago public examinations were mainly designed to discriminate, and paper-setters were criticized if the results produced a narrow rather than a broad range of marks. GCSE examinations are now supposed to be much more criterion-referenced, with performance criteria published for each grade in all subjects. These criteria are intended to be helpful for teachers and pupils, so that they know clearly what they have to teach or learn for success in the examinations, and we should not be surprised that grades at GCSE have improved over the years. Instead of welcoming this improvement, however, as more candidates achieve higher standards, many hostile voices are raised in the media each year, complaining about 'grade inflation' and asserting that the examinations must have been too easy. There is no evidence that examination questions have become easier, and the critics may not be aware of assessment grades based on standardized criteria. They would probably be more content with the deliberately discriminating, norm-referenced examinations of earlier times.

Another effect of using more criterion-referencing in public examinations is a change in the perception of pass and fail grades. People who, by now, ought to know better, persist in asking applicants 'How many GCSE passes do you have?' rather than 'What grades have you achieved?' Grades A–C are all too often referred to as 'passes', with the implication that D and below are 'fail' grades. Pass and fail should be related to the level of grades required for particular purposes. The skills and abilities needed to achieve a D grade at GCSE may be entirely suitable for appointment to a large number of jobs or for admission to many courses in further education.

ISSUES OF REPORTING GRADES

Apart from interpreting grades as achieved under criterion- or norm-referencing, there is the issue of the single grade itself. Grades are usually awarded as a result of tests designed to reveal candidates' proficiency and competence in a variety of skills, knowledge and understanding. In a well-designed test it should be possible to attribute marks for success in attaining particular objectives such as knowledge and understanding of the content of a syllabus, or practical skills, or the ability to write a coherent essay. In such cases, a more full and clear picture of the candidate's capabilities should surely be revealed by recording the marks and grades achieved under the different objectives, rather than aggregating them into a single grade. There have been requests over the years for more detailed recording of achievement in specified skills and abilities, and many schools do use internal 'profile' reports and records of achievement. Regrettably there has not yet been sufficient incentive for the Awarding Bodies to unpack the grades they award in each subject and to reveal the underlying patterns of achievement. Providing a profile of achievements within subjects in public examinations would, of course, cost more, but the gains would be much better informed and realistic discussions with the pupils, parents and other 'users' than is possible using the relatively uninformative single grade for each subject.

ISSUES ON CHOOSING TECHNIQUES OF ASSESSMENT

An extensive range of techniques is available for assessment. These are the means through which pupils/candidates try to demonstrate what they 'know, understand and can do'. The choices for assessors are shown in Table 3.2.

Table 3.2: Choices for assessors

Techniques	Examples
Objective tests	Multiple-choice items
	Adding single words to gaps in sentences
Short answer questions	Structured questions
Extended writing	Essays
	Accounts of experience, e.g. in practical work
Comprehension exercises	Questions based on a substantial portion of text; may include précis task
Projects and extended assignments	Use of databases, questionnaires, surveys, field-work
Practical work and performance	Based on work in laboratory or studio; includes short 'can-do' tests for particular skills
Oral assessment	Mainly in languages including English; often in other subjects as part of project assessment

An *objective question* or *item* is assumed to have only one correct answer. There is a special vocabulary for multiple-choice items. Here is an example of an item from a test used for university entrance:

> *Choose the word or phrase that is most nearly opposite in meaning to the word INFERNAL.*
>
> *(a) exquisite (b) frigid (c) ephemeral (d) mortal (e) celestial*

The section containing the information and instruction or question at the beginning is known as the *stem*. The *alternative* answers are divided into the single correct answer, known as the *key*, with the others described as *distractors*. (In the item above, the key is (e).)

Objective items are at their most valid in assessment requiring factual recall and rule-governed reasoning. Many questions may be answered in a fairly short time and the appropriate objectives and content of a section of a syllabus or course can be well covered. Their validity is much lower for testing higher cognitive abilities (such as analysis, synthesis or judgement) as these abilities are not effectively revealed in the exercise of choosing from a list of predetermined answers. The practicability of multiple-choice items is also somewhat limited, as setters are often challenged to find up to four plausible distractors. Examination Boards have to keep large banks of multiple-choice items for use and reuse. The great strength of objective items, however, is their high reliability as there is rarely disagreement about the answers. This commends them to assessment systems in many countries where reliability and ease of marking are of particular concern.

The major issue in the use of all the other techniques is that of reliability. As soon as an opinion is required about a candidate's answer, there is the possibility of different marks being awarded by different assessors. This issue of subjectivity and reliability is understandably raised most often in the more creative areas such as English essays or performance in Drama, Art or Music, but also occurs in assessment of investigative and project work in other subjects. Assessors, particularly in the Awarding Bodies, try to improve reliability by insisting upon detailed marking schemes and criteria for grades, using more than one marker for each script and a variety of moderation techniques. There has to be a compromise with practicability, however, as all improvements towards reliability incur time and financial costs.

Validity is also an issue for examination papers consisting of essays. Only a limited sample of a course's content may be covered by essay questions, even in a 2 to 3 hour paper. There is concern too that gender bias may affect the validity of assessment styles as, for example, females tend to achieve higher standards in questions requiring extended answers and males tend to perform more successfully in objective items.

Assessors in different subjects recognize that there are these issues of validity, reliability, practicability and bias in designing tests and examinations, and usually make sensible compromises by choosing a suitably mixed variety of techniques.

FURTHER INFORMATION

Relevant and recent information about developments in national assessment may be found in the websites of the main institutions involved in public examinations.

The Qualifications and Curriculum Authority (QCA) was established in 1997 to advise the Secretary of State for Education on all aspects of the school curriculum and as a regulatory body for public examinations and publicly funded qualifications. The QCA website is http://www.open.gov.uk/qca/.

The Awarding Bodies (formed by mergers of the older Examination Boards and Vocational Bodies) in England are:

- Assessment and Qualifications Alliance (AQA) at http://www.aqa.org.uk/.
- Edexcel at http://www.edexcel.org.uk/.
- Oxford, Cambridge and RSA Examinations (OCR) at http://www.ocr.org.uk/.

In Northern Ireland, the regulatory and awarding body is:

- Council for the Curriculum, Examinations and Assessment (CCEA) at http://www.ccea.org.uk/.

In Scotland the regulatory and awarding body is:

- Scottish Qualifications Authority (SQA) at http://www.sqa.org.uk/.

In Wales the regulatory body is:

- ACCAC at http:// www.accac.org.uk/.
- The awarding body is the Welsh Joint Education Committee (WJEC) at http://www.wjec.co.uk/.

Chapter 4

Classroom Teaching and Learning

REX WALFORD

INTRODUCTION

'Now what I want is Facts. Teach these boys and girls nothing but Facts. Facts alone are wanted in life. Plant nothing else and root out everything else . . . Stick to Facts, sir!' That was the educational philosophy of Thomas Gradgrind, the schoolmaster in Charles Dickens' *Hard Times,* based on the belief that children's minds were akin to empty vessels. Mr M'Choakumchild, lately trained in one of the earliest of the teacher-training colleges, obediently followed Gradgrind's precepts and poured gallons of Facts into the waiting receptacles. Dickens observes wistfully (at the end of Chapter 2) 'Ah, rather overdone, M'Choakumchild. If he had only learnt a little less, how infinitely better he might have taught much more!' – a danger which still has a message for any who undertake a contemporary postgraduate Initial Teacher Training course.

It is just possible that some new entrants approach a career in teaching in the twenty-first century believing the Gradgrind philosophy. If not – whatever subject they may teach – they have surely realized that it is necessary to have a grasp of some fundamental insights into the way in which children's minds develop and how they learn; together with the most appropriate ways of matching teaching activities and situations to their needs, so that education takes place with common intent.

HOW DO CHILDREN'S MINDS DEVELOP?

The way in which children's minds develop has been a matter of speculation, investigation and theorizing for many decades. In the nineteenth century and at the start of the twentieth, the experimental work of Friedrich Froebel (1782–1852) and Maria Montessori (1870–1952) drew attention in different ways to the importance of providing activity and spontaneity in children's learning. Froebel, a German educationalist, was founder of the kindergarten system and his avowed aim was to allow the mind of the child to grow naturally and through activity; Montessori was the first woman in Italy to receive a medical degree, but was also an educationalist who developed a system of education based on spontaneity of expression and freedom from restraint. The views and practices of these pioneers were in stark contrast to the passive rote-learning of earlier times, and they strongly influenced elementary (later to be called primary) educators, especially the American John Dewey (1859–1952) who saw the essence of education as children involved in constructive play and problem-solving. In later years, this has been characterized as 'enquiry' or 'discovery' learning, and its influence has stretched beyond primary education and into the secondary sector in almost all academic subjects.

Alongside this has been investigation into the way in which children develop their mental and specifically their cognitive faculties. For many years, the most eminent worker and writer in this sphere was Jean Piaget (1896–1980), a Swiss psychologist, whose development of a theory of 'stages of mental development' was based on a series of closely observed empirical experiments carried out under specialized conditions. Piaget's theory is not an overall theory of child development, still less a theory of education, but it linked cognitive development to a series of stages approximately related to age:

- 0–2 years: *the sensory–motor period*, when the infant is combining sensation and movement to construct an initial picture of the world.
- 2–7 years: *the pre-operational period*, when the development of language enables mental structures to be transformed into symbolic ones, and concepts of past and future are formed.
- 7–11 years: *the period of concrete operations*, when children can reason about particular events if they have particular observable examples to work from.
- 11–adulthood: *the period of formal operations*, when there is the development and maturation of logical reasoning, and complex causal relationships can be deduced even if the relevant phenomena are not immediately observable.

Piaget viewed the child as a solitary explorer, regarded language development as little more than a corollary of biologically based maturation, and assumed that the development of thought followed the same basic pattern in all children. His view of the stages of development was thus biologically based.

In more recent times, Piaget's theories have been challenged, notably by the American, Jerome Bruner (1915–). Bruner's work suggested that even very young children could think in a sophisticated way. Some of his experiments suggested that even babies in their cradle were capable of making hypotheses (rather than reacting by instinct) *before* they were capable of language – a significant difference from Piaget's account. Bruner acknowledged that thinking is greatly enriched and facilitated by language but not, in essence, dependent on it. He consequently suggested the possibility of the 'acceleration' of the curriculum, in the belief that 'any topic can be taught to any child at any age' as long as it is presented in appropriate ways. Associated with this was the idea of the 'spiral curriculum': the notion that a curriculum for a subject or topic should centre around a set of key ideas which are revisited in successively more complex ways.

Like Piaget, however, Bruner also developed theories about stages – but stages of how we represent the environment to ourselves when we are learning. Bruner's stages were not tied to chronological age. Bruner's first stage is 'enactive representation', in which certain commonly performed actions (eating, riding a bicycle) become automatic through the development of a kind of 'memory bank' in the muscles and relevant areas of the brain. The second stage is 'iconic representation' in which we use connected imagery (e.g. spatial patterns) to help us remember what we have experienced (e.g. the names of people in a group). The third stage is 'symbolic representation' in which the connection between underlying reality and representation is (and is understood to be) detached and arbitrary (e.g. a chemical formula, a map, a word), but we nevertheless understand the link and its meaning, and accept it.

Piaget's ideas were also challenged by the Russian psychologist Lev Vygotsky (1896–1934) who developed theories about language in relation to children's thinking, and of the importance of cultural and social factors in developing cognition. Vygotsky believed that even the youngest child is a *social* being and that it is through interaction with others that the child develops an understanding of self and a capacity for thought. Vygotsky's three key stages of 'development' were: instinct; learning by training (or reflex conditioning); and learning through the intellect.

For Vygotsky, the relationship between teacher and learner, and between learners and other learners, was the key to promoting more effective learning. The area between what could be achieved by independent learning and what could be achieved with the help and guidance of the teacher (or other more experienced helper) he called 'the zone of proximal development'. He also believed that *language* played a vital part in the development of thought and was not merely a passive or automatic reflection of non-linguistic thought processes. Thus talk and socializing were key factors in Vygotsky's principles of education.

Benjamin Bloom and his co-workers developed an 'educational taxonomy' in the 1970s which identified and clarified what they called different 'domains' of learning – the cognitive (concerned with levels of intellectual learning); the affective (concerned with feelings and values); and the psychomotor (concerned with physical skills, such as putting a ball in a netball net). Bloom's work has in practice been most used in relation to the cognitive domain and has led to a greater understanding for teachers of how to plan classroom tasks and also how to evaluate learning.

His 'ladder' of cognitive attributes begins with 'remembering' and continues upwards with 'comprehending' and 'application' (applying material in a new circumstances). These precede 'analysis', 'synthesis' and, at the top of the ladder, 'evaluation'. Teachers who design learning tasks with care find cuewords which can indicate the level of thinking required from students. For example, 'Give an account of . . .' is a straightforward task which requires mainly the remembering and comprehending of material; 'Evaluate . . .' is clearly a task requiring a higher level of thinking, one which will, in all probability, encompass all the other levels of thinking below it. 'Discuss' – a favourite enigmatic cue word of examiners at all levels – invites a student to choose which level of thinking they think is appropriate to the question in hand . . . and then see if the examiners agree!

Following on from this, the work of D. Kolb and others, on the differing 'styles' in which individuals learn most comfortably, illuminates this area further. Kolb identifies 'accommodators', 'divergers', 'convergers'and 'assimilators' as his main categories – see his book *Experiential Learning* (1984) for further details.

We know that some people appear to be more *creative thinkers* than others; correspondingly some are better at puzzling through problems, using logic. For instance, consider these two tasks:

1. 'Brothers and sisters have I none, but that man's father is my father's son.' Who am I?
2. How many uses can you think of for a brick?

It is likely that you will be much more 'comfortable' with one than the other – perhaps those who are scientifically and mathematically inclined can solve the first problem easily; those who have studied in the creative subjects may find the second task more to their liking. Edward de Bono has written a number of popular and readable books which have illuminated the different ways in which people think (and don't think) and the ways in which more creative problem-solving might be encouraged and developed.

Good teachers take account of these differences in 'learning styles' in lesson planning and teaching, ensuring that they do not set the same type of learning activity all the time, nor unduly value one type to the exclusion of all the others.

WHAT CONTENT SHOULD WE TEACH?

Keiran Egan has pointed out that schoolteachers need to know not only how children's minds work, but what is the most appropriate content and style to use at each stage of their development. His theory of educational development links both and identifies successively:

1. The 'mythic' stage (during which children respond best to stories).
2. The 'romantic' stage (during which pupils are keen to learn facts, and will absorb great amounts of information).
3. The 'philosophic' stage (during which children become interested in developing generalizations, and principles).
4. The 'ironic' stage (the sign of a 'mature' mind, during which the focus shifts to the exploration of those instances which do not obey the usual rules).

In Egan's opinion, children who enter secondary school have usually at least reached the second stage, though some may not progress much further. These stages are curiously named, but they may well, nevertheless, remind you of the interests and enthusiasms which you had at different stages of your own education. They are a pointer for the development of teaching materials and also for the setting of appropriate tasks in lessons and for homework. Egan's work reminds us too that what enthuses and interests an adult does not necessarily do the same for a 12 year old, and that teachers need to both select and interpret subject material in different ways for different age groups and ability groups. The advent of a closely specified National Curriculum removes some of the options from this debate, but the National Curriculum in England and Wales is only a basic prescription and not an encompassing umbrella for learning; moreover the revisions initiated from September 2000 will further reduce the extent of detailed prespecification in many subject areas.

HOW DO WE MOTIVATE PUPILS SO THAT THEY LEARN EFFECTIVELY?

The pessimists in education (Mr Gradgrind prominent) argue that children must be coerced into educational tasks; that the rule of fear is the only effective weapon for the schoolteacher to use. John Holt (1969) has eloquently recorded the results of such a system in *How Children Fail*. The progressive diminution of the unquestioning acceptance of authority is a potent argument against this position, a diminution achieved, in large part, because of the fruits of education itself. 'Do it because I say so' has now only a limited effectiveness in most schools – and that because of respect for the speaker, rather than fear. Such respect, increasingly, is earned rather than imposed.

The more significant debate in this area is between those who favour systems of extrinsic motivation, that is to say, providing a system of rewards and satisfactions as an 'external' response to good or successful work, and those who believe that intrinsic motivation is more powerful.

B. F. Skinner (1904–1990) is the most celebrated proponent of extrinsic mechanisms of 'positive or negative reinforcement' and his 'behaviourism' has led, *inter alia*, to the development of programmed learning (with its immediate feedback mechanisms) and also to schemes in which 'house points' or small privileges of various kinds are offered as a routine incentive to those who do well or work hard.

Psychologists like J. McV. Hunt (1961 and 1971) take the view that there is more virtue and more ultimate success in selecting and designing tasks so that there is a ready acquiescence from the learners – in other words, seeking to obtain the goodwill and co-operation of pupils so that they themselves are self-motivated to achieve without seeking extrinsic rewards. Many teachers see intrinsic motivation as a desirable goal, but a key issue is whether *all* school learning can be made intrinsically interesting. Some would argue that pupils need to achieve certain goals (e.g. learning their tables) which cannot be made intrinsically appealing; others argue that there are always ways of 'dressing-up' material so that pupils will want to learn.

WHAT STRATEGIES AND METHODS SHOULD WE USE TO TEACH?

An understanding of learning and motivational insights needs to be buttressed with an understanding of pedagogy (i.e. teaching methods) and – a vital third part of the equation – a corresponding ability to perform well so that the chosen strategy successfully delivers the educational goods.

Early writers about education assumed a one-to-one relationship; Rousseau's *Emile* was postulated on a teacher with a single scholar, and this was a preferred style of education for the very rich until quite recently (the 'governess', the 'tutor'). As formal education became a mass experience, however, the development of schools in which teachers had classes of dozens of pupils was inevitable, and rules of management and control developed.

There has, however, long been a radical school of thought which argues that schooling should not be compulsory, and/or that it should be based on a negotiated rather than an imposed curriculum. Schools such as the independent Summerhill in Suffolk, originally run by A. S. Neill and his family, and the state-funded Countesthorpe College in Leicestershire (for a period in the 1960s and 1970s) have sought to make this a convincing reality, but it has never been a model seriously followed by any but a handful of schools.

In the 1970s, the writings of Ivan Illich and Paulo Freire encouraged debate about 'de-schooling' and the merits of informal education beyond school buildings and in community settings. The current initiatives about lifelong learning and (for example) certain versions of the idea that the state should give everyone vouchers to spend on whatever education they wish, when they wish, are offspring of this simmering debate about the appropriate nature of educational institutions.

A second strand of the debate (also manifest in the debate about selective and comprehensive schooling) relates to the *groupings* in which pupils are taught. The tripartite system (grammar, technical, secondary modern) established by the 1944 Education Act (discussed in Chapter 1) was replaced by a gradual 'comprehensivization' of schools in the 1970s and 1980s, and there grew up a quite widespread belief that teaching in 'mixed ability' classes brought social benefits and little educational disadvantage. In the last ten years the debate has intensified, as a perception has grown that the most able pupils are not fully stretched in mixed ability classes and that the overall educational achievement of the school population in the UK gives cause for concern. For many schools there is now a live issue about the balance of 'streaming', 'banding' or 'setting' as alternatives to mixed ability grouping – and a judgement to be made over whether maximum educational achievement should be given priority over social objectives.

The third strand of this debate leads us back to Mr Gradgrind – what *methods and approaches* is it best to use, and are these the same for every subject, or should we expect there to be more rote-learning in (say) Modern Languages and Maths, than in History or English?

A radical (and highly readable) critique of traditional methods was made in an influential book by Neil Postman and Charles Weingartner, first published in 1969, and it related to a perceived change in the necessary philosophy and objectives of schooling. If, they argued, we now need schools to prepare students for the future in a highly dynamic and changing world, students will need flexibility of mind and the development of an independent capability, not merely the capacity to 'guess what the teacher is thinking when a question is asked'. The move which they advocated towards more enquiry methods, the use of experiential learning (games, role-play, etc.), group discussion, problem-solving and project work, gained credibility in many subject areas. It was underpinned by an optimistic belief that the 'basics' would continue to be picked up by an osmotic process as pupils worked on genuinely interesting and involving exercises. This turned out to be unjustified in many cases.

The pendulum has swung again in the last few years, and the current educational concern of all main political parties in the UK (and of Ofsted, the inspectional arm of government) as we enter the twenty-first century seems focused on the acquisition of basic skills and an encouragement to return to more 'tried and tested' traditional methods. Thus there is now renewed advocacy of the teaching of reading by phonics, and the learning of number tables in primary schools; and also of whole-class interactional teaching and expositional methods in both secondary and primary schools. It might be argued that, in the 1970s and 1980s, process and experience became more important in schools than product and that the transmission of knowledge was undesirably downplayed – almost to the point of extinction by some teachers. The current dominant view suggests that there must be a balance for pupils between acquiring basic information on the one hand and developing skills and desirable attitudes and values, through which it is put to good use, on the other.

WHAT CHANGES MAY THERE BE IN THE FUTURE?

The use of information and communications technology has yet to be fully integrated into classroom teaching and learning, despite the 'honeymoon' period of the late 1990s. ICT enthusiasts optimistically predict radical shifts in learning patterns, but these are unlikely to materialize until there are computers in every classroom and not merely in specialist rooms on which there are necessarily limitations on use. Extreme prophecies suggest that the school itself may one day become redundant as an institution, as the Internet increases the power of home learning; but it is more likely that the social attraction of schools, the quest for community life and the desire for personal interaction as part of learning will remain powerful and conserving factors. Unless a new era of Gradgrindery emerges, classrooms, schools and teachers are likely to remain enduring parts of the educational landscape for the foreseeable future.

Chapter 5

Use of Language in the School and Classroom

GABRIELLE CLIFF HODGES

LANGUAGE VARIETY IN SCHOOL

In school, students encounter and use a wide range of language:

- vocabulary peculiar to school, e.g. 'Principal', 'Head of Year', 'assembly', 'break', 'tutor time', 'PSE', 'homework diary', 'detention';
- vocabulary in specialist subjects with the same word sometimes having different meanings in different lessons, e.g. 'space' used in Maths, Science, Art;
- vocabulary associated with different technologies, e.g. 'pen', 'book', 'mouse', 'cursor', 'screen';
- a range of language types, e.g. 'instruction', 'coercion', 'sympathy', 'discipline';
- a range of languages, dialects and accents.

This diversity of language use is often taken for granted by teachers and students alike.

However, close observation of language in the classroom shows just how complex students' achievements are as they move between different languages, or between the spoken and written word, or formal and informal language in different contexts, for example: with peers in the playground; in tutor time or assembly; in lessons; in the dining hall, the library, the computer room; in the school council or the drama club. Much of this language appears to be assimilated by students simply through using it on a daily basis. But this is not always the case. A student may not have understood subject-specific terminology or usage, or may not speak or write very much at all, and therefore misses opportunities to experiment with language, to learn or understand. There is much that teachers can do to help develop students' language, for example by planning work which involves wide-ranging language use, and teaching students explicitly about it.

In the past there has been a tendency in secondary schools for language study to be seen as the domain of the English department despite long-standing calls for people to realize that every teacher is a teacher of English because every teacher is a teacher in English. *English for Ages 5–16* (DES 1989), commonly referred to as the Cox report, which formed the basis for English in the National Curriculum, contained a paragraph which summed up well what language is, what it does and why *every* teacher should pay attention to it:

> Language is a system of sounds, meanings and structures with which we make sense of the world around us. It functions as a tool of thought; as a means of social organisation; as a repository and means of transmission of knowledge; as the raw material of literature; and as the creator and sustainer – or destroyer – of human relationships. It changes inevitably over time and, as change is not uniform, from place to place. Because language is a fundamental part of being human, it is an important aspect of a person's sense of self; because it is a fundamental feature of any community, it is an important aspect of a person's sense of social identity. (DES 1989, para. 6.18)

If language is a fundamental part of being human, then it is the proper concern of *all* teachers. The National Curriculum goes some way towards recognizing this in the following statement:

> Pupils should be taught in all subjects to express themselves correctly and appropriately and to read accurately and with understanding. Since Standard English, spoken and written, is the predominant language in which knowledge and skills are taught and learned, pupils should be taught to recognise and use Standard English.
> - In *writing* they should be taught to use correct spelling and punctuation and follow grammatical conventions. They should also be taught to organise their writing in logical and coherent forms.
> - In *speaking*, pupils should be taught to use language precisely and cogently.
> - Pupils should be taught to *listen* to others, and respond and build on their ideas and views constructively.
> - In *reading*, pupils should be taught strategies to help them read with understanding, locate and use information, follow a process or argument and summarise, synthesise and adapt what they learn from their reading.
> Pupils should be taught the *technical and specialist vocabulary* of subjects and how to use and spell these words. They should be taught to use the patterns of language vital to understanding and expression in different subjects. These include the construction of sentences, paragraphs and texts which are often used in a subject, *e.g. language to express causality, chronology, logic, exploration, hypothesis, comparison, and how to ask questions and develop argument.* (DfEE 1999, p. 11)

Likewise, the National Literacy Strategy (DfEE 1997), with its target of 80 per cent of 11 year olds achieving National Curriculum Level 4 by 2002, recognizes the contribution to be made by all teachers, not just language specialists. Primary schools are strongly urged (but not legally obliged) to adopt the detailed Framework for Teaching with its daily literacy hour as part of the overall strategy. Many secondary schools, mindful of the possible impact of the strategy on their incoming Year 7 students, have set about reconsidering how literacy can best be developed across the whole curriculum, although in perhaps more flexible, less prescriptive ways than those enjoined by the National Literacy Strategy.

If language is a fundamental part of being human, then language learning and development is also the entitlement of *all* students. Teachers should, therefore, from the first, consider the different needs and language strengths of *all* students in their classes. These will vary, depending for example on whether students are monolingual, bilingual or multilingual; whether they have recently arrived from abroad and are learning English as an additional language; whether they attend language classes out of school. Levels of specialist support for those learning English as an additional language will vary considerably from school to school, as will school policies on inclusion or withdrawal. It is highly likely, however, that most teachers, some or all of the time, will find themselves working in multilingual classrooms. As Josie Levine argues, they therefore need to ask themselves a fundamental question:

> What do we need to know about additional language learning/subject knowledge/English mother-tongue teaching that will help us to teach our subject/class better? Such a question suggests that the intentions of teacher and the needs of their pupils are about to overlap in more fruitful ways than before. More fruitful for the children's learning and language and their social development, and more fruitful in furthering the development of teaching styles that are about the language, social and learning needs of all children. (Levine, in Meek 1996, p. 53)

A further, challenging question about multilingual classrooms, again posed by Josie Levine, is: 'What are the tools of hospitality?' (*ibid.*, p. 53). It is a question she proceeds to answer in ways which are of immediate practical relevance to the classroom. Classrooms which are 'hospitable to diversity' are those in which, for example, students are encouraged to work collaboratively, take risks and join in, learning about the language demands of specific classrooms and subject areas as teachers or peers model the language for them, hearing how different questions are framed so that they can learn to use them for their own particular ends. Students should hear, as often as possible, 'the tunes and rhythms of English' read aloud, whether from a class novel, a newspaper article, a passage from a geography textbook, a report on a science experiment, instructions for a game in physical education. Students should be encouraged to draw on their knowledge about languages in which they *are* already fluent and experienced to help them develop their skills in English in ways which do not diminish the significance of the first language.

Working in any classroom involves the teacher thinking about differentiation in as many ways as possible. Quite apart from the students' diversity of language needs, they have other needs relating to their knowledge, their understanding of the concepts of a subject, their skills and aptitudes, their motivation and their preferred learning styles (Hall 1995). The use of a variety of teaching styles and resources is as important as ever, as is the careful consideration which must be given to the demands of any task set and the support required for students to be able to achieve an outcome at an appropriate level.

Mindful of the importance of differentiation, the revised Orders for the National Curriculum contain a new general statement about inclusion which highlights teachers' obligation to provide effective learning opportunities and challenges to meet the diversity of students' needs. Ways to assist all students to achieve the highest standards are suggested, including those who exceed the expected level of attainment within any subject, those for whom English is an additional language, and students with Special Educational Needs.

LANGUAGE AND LEARNING

Whoever, or wherever, they teach, teachers need to understand the integral relationship between language, thought and learning. The theories of Vygotsky (Vygotsky 1978, 1986) are helpful in this respect. Vygotsky argues that young children learn to think by talking with others, by engaging in social and cultural practices which enable them to 'grow into the intellectual life of those around them' (Vygotsky, 1978, p. 88). Later, speech divides into two particular strands: 'communicative' speech which we use to communicate with other people, and 'egocentric' speech which we use to communicate with ourselves. In the early stages, egocentric speech is audible; but it eventually becomes silent 'inner' speech with its own idiosyncrasies of grammar, for individual thinking. (Occasionally, however, especially when faced with a complex challenge, e.g. learning how to use a new piece of computer software, we may talk aloud to ourselves again as a way of coming to know and understand how the software works.) Inner speech has different patterns from communicative speech: with inner speech, speaker and listener are the same person, so there is much that can be taken for granted. When we use communicative speech, the aim is to be understood by another person, so we have to make our ideas more explicit. Inner speech, therefore, is fundamentally different from communicative speech because it serves a different purpose. However, although inner and communicative speech are different they are nevertheless related, and it is the dynamic between them which, according to Vygotsky, enables intellectual development. It is therefore very important for teachers to have some understanding of this two-way process and how that understanding can be harnessed to help children become more effective learners.

Over the last few decades, researchers and teachers have studied the use of language in the classroom ever more closely. They have focused on the process of students' learning and the part played by different kinds of language: community dialects, mother tongues, spoken standard English. They have looked at the language for task-setting or asking questions. They have observed the impact of the context and environment on teachers' and students' use of language. They have noted what linguistic difference is made by the relative urgency of the problems being solved. New understandings have subsequently emerged about the crucial influence of exploratory talk on cognitive development, and how students talk themselves into understanding as they speculate, question, hypothesize, argue and negotiate.

In the late 1980s and early 1990s, the National Oracy Project (Norman 1992) helped to disseminate more widely ideas about the role of talk in learning and to influence classroom practice. For example, teachers began to plan specific small-group activities which involved students talking to solve problems, analyse texts, and debate controversial issues. They made use of activities such as role play as an alternative way of exploring subject knowledge, be it in Science, History or personal and social education. Whether students were learning *through* talk or learning *about* talk, it was clear that there could be no justifiable return to classrooms which were predominantly silent.

Students were taught *about* talk, teachers making explicit what students already knew implicitly; for example, that spoken language is affected by the context and purpose of the communication and by the audience to whom it is addressed, and why people alternate between speaking in Standard English or in a community dialect, between one language and another.

Given the complexity and importance of language in the classroom, all ITT trainees need to ask themselves the question: 'What, as a teacher, do I need to know about language?'

KNOWLEDGE ABOUT LANGUAGE

Grammar

In order to teach effectively about language it is necessary to have a clear understanding about grammar. Grammar is the system by which, in any language, words are formed and linked together to make meaning. Grammar includes the stock of words from which we choose (vocabulary or lexis); the forms of words (morphology), e.g. 'run' or 'ran', 'stop' or 'stopped'; the order of words (syntax), e.g. 'I was walking through the woods when I saw a fox' or 'I saw a fox as I was walking through the woods'. Any variety of English, whether Standard English or one of its dialects, is distinguishable by specific features of its grammar and vocabulary.

According to Ron Carter:

Standard English may be defined as that variety of English which is usually used in print and which is normally taught in schools and to non-native speakers using the language. It is also the variety which is normally spoken by educated people and used in news broadcasts and other similar situations. It is especially characterised by a rich and extensive vocabulary developed over centuries for a range of functions ... Though it has been extensively described and codified, Standard English is not an homogeneous entity; it is subject to historical change and variation across the world. (Carter 1995, p. 145)

Dialects spoken in different parts of the UK have their own different but equally systematic grammars and vocabularies. Indeed, it is by distinctive features of grammar and vocabulary that different dialects are identifiable, as you will discover if you try to identify which regional dialects the following sentences come from:

- They've wrote me three letters.
- I just ignores people like that.
- You're going, isn't it?
- How are y'all feeling today?
- We didnae think o' that.
- We couldn't see nowt.
- Who is it you'll be wanting?
- Can I give youse a lift?
- Why they do that?
- We was walking down the road.   (Taken from Crystal 1996, p. 25)

As teachers it is important for us to know the grammar and vocabulary of dialects in the areas where we teach in order to be able to distinguish between when students are using the grammar and vocabulary of a local dialect or when genuine grammatical mistakes are being made in spoken or written Standard English. Students need to learn the advantages of using Standard English in certain contexts and be in a position to choose when and why to do so. For example, a student doing work experience as a receptionist will need to use Standard English to ensure that clients from anywhere in the country or the world can understand clearly; when at home with family or friends, the same student will probably use a local dialect as a mark of greater informality, familiarity and intimacy.

Another crucial distinction which teachers need to be able to make is between the grammar of spoken and written language. As Katherine Perera points out:

There are two important points to be made that concern the nature of speech on the one hand, and the nature of writing on the other. First, there is a fairly widely held but mistaken view that speech is some kind of careless or sloppy version of writing. This view leads people to make judgements of speech that are inappropriate because they derive from the written standard ... Secondly, it is necessary to realise that written language is not merely a transcription of speech; so learning to read and write means not just learning to make and decode letter shapes but also acquiring new forms of language. Some difficulties in reading spring from the language itself rather than from the written code, because there are some grammatical constructions which are common in writing but which occur very rarely in speech. (Perera 1987, pp. 17–19)

Spoken-language grammar is strongly influenced by the fact that the speaker is almost always in the presence of the listener (telephone and radio, however, being two of the few exceptions). The presence of the listener and the spontaneity of most spoken language changes the grammatical ways in which meaning is conveyed. For example, speakers:

- make use of stress patterns, pitch, speed and volume so listeners can hear what is meant;
- use gestures and body language to supplement what they say;
- repeat themselves, make false starts, hesitate, trail off without the listener necessarily losing the thread;
- interrupt each other or take turns;
- link infinite numbers of clauses together (a pattern sometimes known as 'chaining') rather than speaking in sentences with clearly defined beginnings and endings.

However fluent and careful spoken language may sound, its grammar is often very different from the grammar of written language. Look, for example, at the following transcript of a section of a Radio 5 commentary on the final game of a tennis match at Wimbledon in 1995:

Sanchez Vicario onto the Graf backhand and that is just inside the baseline the return and a forehand from Graf and a forehand reply higher from Sanchez Vicario now Sanchez Vicario pulled onto her backhand she goes across court with it but is beaten by the reply.

A tape recording of this extract reveals the commentator speaking at great speed in order to keep up with the pace of the point being played. His excited intonation conveys the spirit of the match to his listeners. His elliptical, telegraphic style is entirely appropriate for the context and purpose. If he used lengthier phrases and clauses he would quickly fall behind each shot. Notice, also, the unusual word order in the first two lines – 'that is just inside the baseline the return' – where one might expect 'the return is just inside the baseline'. In tennis, winning the point depends upon whether the ball lands inside or outside the baseline. Here, then, the commentator gives his listeners the crucial information first ('inside the baseline') and then the additional information ('the return').

This is an example of spoken-language grammar which it would be misleading to describe as wrong. It is, however, different from what one might expect to read in a newspaper report on the match next day. Such a report might include the following sentences:

> Sanchez Vicario played the return to Graf's backhand and it landed just inside the baseline. A forehand from Graf led to an even higher forehand reply from Sanchez Vicario. Sanchez Vicario was pulled onto her backhand, going across court with it, but was beaten by the reply.

Teachers can draw students' attention to such differences and thus assist them in making distinctions, in their own writing, between spoken and written grammatical structures.

Much of the writing students undertake in school is expected to be in Standard English. Students whose local dialect is similar to Standard English are at an advantage here. Nevertheless, even if a student's writing contains a number of errors, it is unusual for many of those errors to be grammatical. Instead they may involve the following:

- difficulty in making the transition from spoken to written, e.g. 'Well, when Queen Elizabeth came to the throne ...';
- oddities of style, e.g. 'I hope you will look on my application gladly';
- incorrect use of a correctly spelt word e.g. 'I put the book over their';
- misconceptions about punctuation, e.g. 'I went home, I had my tea'.

If they are grammatical then it may simply be a case of using local dialect grammar when Standard English was appropriate, for example 'we was' rather than 'we were'.

It is therefore helpful if, when correcting students' work, teachers consider any errors carefully, deciding whether they are to do with grammar, style, spelling or punctuation, and offer precise guidance for learning how to put them right, rather than loosely condemning the work as 'ungrammatical'.

Oracy

ITT trainees are often anxious about talk in classrooms, especially if they remember working in virtually silent classrooms when they were at school. They may have a tendency to equate silence with good discipline. It can, therefore, be very illuminating to observe closely how spoken language is used in order to understand its potential. If classroom activities are well planned you can observe the extent to which they provide opportunities for cognitive development through communicative speech, motivating students to hypothesize or predict, compare and contrast, express and justify feelings or viewpoints, consider the opinions of others, organize, interpret and represent ideas and information, ask questions and think aloud. You can also analyse how such planned activities support the language development of all students, including those who are not fluent in English.

You can observe the extent to which the teacher's own use of language makes a difference to students' learning, for example through careful questioning. There are two main kinds of questions: closed questions which attempt to elicit one single correct answer ('In what year did Queen Victoria die?') and open questions which attempt to elicit a range of responses, ideas or hypotheses ('Is 16 the best age to end compulsory schooling?'). A teacher's choice of questions depends upon the planned learning objectives: do they wish to discover what students already know or do they want them to talk themselves into understanding?

Reading

Reading forms a very considerable part of the secondary school curriculum and it is important for teachers to find ways to develop their students' reading skills. It is necessary to find out and build on what students already know and can do. Students for whom English is an additional language may be very fluent readers in other languages. We need to know as much as possible about how and what they read in other languages to ensure that they are offered reading material and levels of support which are appropriate.

Finding out what the students know and can do may best be done by asking them directly and taking a genuine interest in what they choose to read for themselves in their own time. Their answers may be very illuminating (Hall and Coles 1999). But there are other ways to find out, too: observing students informally in the classroom, library or resources centre and noting what kinds of reading sustain their concentration for the longest periods of time; analysing their ability to annotate or make notes from reading material; recording their preferences for different kinds of texts, for example electronic or print, visual or diagrammatic; reading their records from previous schools; looking at their results from statutory and published reading tests (e.g. cognitive abilities tests or NFER group reading tests). Listening carefully and systematically to them reading aloud may be revealing. However, any one of these approaches alone is unlikely to be sufficient. Reading is a multi-faceted process and it therefore cannot be adequately assessed by one method alone.

Many secondary schools are currently exploring different schemes for what is known as 'reading intervention'. For example Paired Reading, where a less experienced reader is paired up with a more experienced (often older) reader to read together on a regular basis, is one of a number of intensive, systematic schemes designed to help students whose reading is below the level deemed necessary to cope with the demands of the secondary school curriculum.

Clubs, special reading events and literacy summer schools are also being established in the hope that they will encourage inexperienced readers to read more and to raise their standards of literacy. Research evidence about the effectiveness of these kinds of additional (rather than integral) strategies remains, however, somewhat ambivalent. (e.g. Sainsbury *et al.* 1997). Nevertheless, ITT trainees need to find out what literacy strategies are being used in their placement schools but they also need to ask relevant questions about how far such strategies substantially influence students' learning and what research evidence exists to support any claims being made. What is meant by the term 'literacy'? Upon what model of literacy is the school's policy for raising standards based? How far are students encouraged to become literate citizens who (according to the final report of the Advisory Group on Education for Citizenship and the Teaching of Democracy in Schools) have the ability to 'make a reasoned argument both verbally and in writing ... to use modern media and technology critically to gather information ...to recognise forms of manipulation and persuasion'? (Advisory Group on Citizenship 1998, p. 44). Are students people whose literacy offers them (in the words of Gunther Kress) the potential to play a critical, innovative, productive part in society, locally and globally? Are they being prepared by the teaching of literacy across the curriculum 'not just to cope, but to control their circumstances'? (Kress 1995, p. 18).

Writing

Students undertake a great deal of writing in schools. It is interesting to analyse when and how writing contributes to students' learning. The National Writing Project which was set up in the 1980s yielded extremely valuable insights into the nature of the writing process and the implications of this knowledge for teachers and students. Many different factors affect the writing process, so when students are asked to write, it is important to consider things like audience, purpose, genre and whole text structure and to assess students' achievements accordingly. Consider, for example, a task involving writing a letter of complaint to a local councillor about refuse collection and recycling arrangements. Will students be sufficiently familiar with the vocabulary of waste disposal? Will all the students in the class be fully aware of the discourse structure of such a letter – that is, how the shape and language of the letter is affected, even determined, by the power relationship between a councillor and an ordinary member of the public? Students' writing will need to acknowledge that the letter is:

- addressed to a councillor rather than a close friend;
- in the form of a complaint rather than congratulatory;
- a personal letter rather than a letter intended for publication;
- a letter rather than a newspaper article, etc.

Their choice of vocabulary and syntax will also affect the way the letter is received. How the letter is finally judged by the teacher will depend on whether it is a draft version which is being formatively assessed or the final version being summatively assessed. Another consideration will be whether it is handwritten or word-processed and the different effects intended and achieved by one format rather than another. What appears, on the surface, to be a relatively straightforward task, is revealed to be a complex affair.

Careful planning, teaching and assessment are therefore of the essence.

It is always important to consider the learning objectives for any piece of writing a student is asked to undertake, however apparently simple. For example, if notes are to be made, how is students' learning affected by whether the notes are copied, dictated or constructed by the students themselves? Have the students been taught how to make effective notes? Can they see a clear purpose for doing so? What techniques have they learnt to enhance the structure and layout of notes? In short, as teachers we should avoid taking the writing process for granted.

We need to consider what problems or misunderstandings may arise from setting a piece of written work, and offer appropriate structured support and guidance. In particular, given the very different stages of writing development achieved within most classes of secondary students, even if they are setted rather than mixed ability, we need to differentiate the work to meet as precisely as possible the needs of individual students. Some students may welcome the support of writing frames, 'written structures to prompt writing [which seem] to mirror, but develop, the oral promptings that teachers have always instinctively offered to children' (Wray and Lewis 1997, p. 122). The writing frames are skeleton outlines which offer students elements of the finished text, such as sentence openers ('When we lit the Bunsen burner we noticed . . .'), or connectives ('however', 'meanwhile', 'therefore') which help to signal a change of direction in the argument or the start of an alternative viewpoint (*ibid.*). On the other hand, more fluent and experienced writers may welcome the teacher setting them very challenging but achievable targets, for example a tight word limit which forces them to communicate their ideas as succinctly as possible, or a requirement to explore an idea from a number of differing viewpoints, not just their own. Either way, the teacher must think through carefully the implications of the task set and the learning objectives against which it will be assessed.

CONCLUSION

Teachers need to be aware of the potential for students' use of language in the classroom to influence their cognitive development as well as their acquisition and communication of concepts and knowledge. To that end they need to plan for students to talk and listen, read and write for a range of purposes in a variety of contexts to give them the opportunity to develop. Teachers need to ensure that knowledge about language is made explicit, whenever appropriate, so that students understand how language works, are aware of the choices available to them and are confident in whatever uses they make of it.

Part II

Care, Opportunity, Community and Environment

Chapter 6

Pastoral Care and the Work of the Pastoral Tutor

MARY EARL

This chapter can only very briefly introduce you to the vast range of material concerned with understanding adolescence and the relevance of this to the work of the pastoral tutor. What the chapter sets out to do is to ensure that, as pastoral tutors, you are aware of three important things:

- the fact that adolescence is one of several critical psychological and bio-logical developmental stages in the growth of young people, and that successful negotiation of it is also affected by social and cultural factors;
- the fact that this complex transition partly defines the pastoral problems with which we, as tutors, have to deal in secondary education;
- the fact that the nature and the manner in which some of these pastoral problems are presented can lead tutors into difficult 'boundary issues' about which it is best to be forewarned – and hence forearmed.

BIOLOGICAL FACTORS

For some, talking about the pastoral issues related to dealing with pupils in the 11–18 age range mainly means talking about the physical and biological effects of the onset of puberty. Puberty produces the biggest single set of changes to the individual's appearance and, indeed nature, that has happened since they learned to walk, talk and use a potty. At puberty, height and weight rapidly accelerate; secondary sexual characteristics manifest themselves; mature reproductive capacity develops; and there is further growth and dif-ferentiation of cognitive ability. Figures given for the onset of puberty state that the mean age of the menarche (the start of menstruation for girls) is 13 (Year 8), though 15 per cent of girls in the UK now reach puberty before they leave primary school (Year 6). For boys, the average age of puberty is 15 (Year 9/10). It is important to note, though, that the age for the onset of puberty for both boys and girls varies considerably.

Biological change affects every aspect of the adolescent's life. Many of the interactions – psychological, socio-cultural and biological – which occur between young people themselves and between them and us as teachers, during puberty, are influenced by these biological changes. When you take a Year 9 PE lesson such as boys' football, the height, weight and hence strength of the boys in front of you may vary astonishingly. When you take a Year 9 GCSE English or Drama class, you may find there are three to four years of 'maturity difference' in the ways boys and girls choose to engage with the emotional demands of studying a text about love or sexuality. Sometimes this can be irritating. The temptation to say 'Grow up!' to tutees is one that very few of us avoid completely. But we do have to keep in mind the idea that the fact that such anxieties keep re-appearing in our tutees' lives, often seeming completely overwhelming to them, is not entirely their fault!

Adolescents are young people waking up to the realization that they will soon be or are already becoming fully adult, fully capable, biologically, of not only living and breathing and dying, but also of reproducing, of fathering or of mothering. Puberty is not a minor life event and we should not trivialize the developmental problems arising from it.

For adolescents puberty often (not always) means the proliferation of worries – often centring on whether all their new 'body bits' will ever grow, or change, or work, in the appropriate order/at the appropriate time. Dealing with all this anxiety, as a tutor, is not easy. Associated with all this anxiety there often comes a new set of secrecies and embarrassments, around the body and body image. Suddenly the girl in your tutor group who could win a House swimming match for you any day last year won't compete at all and has a period every time there is a match. Everyone seems to be keeping a (very private) diary. Your previously well-adapted, hard-working male tutees' faces break out into acne; their voices break; and their desire to work sinks through the floor. GCSEs are just around the corner. What do you do?

Adolescence and living with anxieties related to puberty is a 'phase' we all know we had to go through ourselves. But tutors need to remember, as the adults they now are, how much adolescents need and expect you to be role models of adulthood for them. This does not mean you have to be perfect but that you need to be able to tolerate tutees' anxieties, quiet them, show them how to manage them if necessary, and be able to help to pilot them through to calmer waters beyond adolescence.

Bullying, teasing, and the miseries of being included or excluded from certain girl and boy 'groupings' due to peer group pressures, are other problems which stem partly from the both the variability and the inevitability of the biological onset of puberty. They may, however, also stem partly from psychological factors affecting adolescence.

PSYCHOLOGICAL FACTORS

When we come to consider what adolescence is, beyond the merely biological, consensus views are surprisingly hard to find.

Psychologists differ widely in their attitude to adolescence. Some have seen it as a near sickness, a difficult but inevitable period of *Sturm und Drang* (Storm and Stress). Teachers must therefore, on this view, expect adolescents to be erratic and 'over the top' emotionally, to be scatty and uncertain about themselves and others – it's all part of adolescence.[1] Others, however, argue that there is no biological law which says the phase of physiological development we call puberty is inevitably accompanied by 'storm and stress'. Some have even said that as a definable life stage, adolescence does not, in any other than the merely biological sense, really exist. It is merely the socio-cultural creation of increasingly leisured, technocratic, liberal Western pluralistic societies.

Developmental psychology however, from Freud to Piaget, Erikson to Kohlberg, suggests that teaching adolescents involves guiding them not through a merely biological phase but through a distinctive psychological, or perhaps more properly, a bio-psychological stage of development. In other words, what is at stake, with the onset of puberty, is not only a change of physical appearance and the onset of the ability to reproduce, but a vast challenge to, and opening of, possibilities for wide-ranging *identity formation*. Erikson, in fact, characterized adolescence as one of eight life stages, each with recognizable tasks to accomplish and each with recognizable problems which could result from not negotiating the transitions adequately (Erikson 1984).

At Erikson's Stage Five (i.e. 12–18 years) the key task is given as *identity versus role confusion*, i.e. it is the task of setting out to make oneself – and of making oneself in a role (or roles), without confusion with the roles of others. Significant influences, unsurprisingly, are peer groups and role models for leadership (including those in neighbourhood and school). It is fairly clear from this what the role of a tutor to pupils in this age group is going to involve. It is also fairly clear what the consequences, for both personal and social development, would be of failing to negotiate the stage effectively.

The fact that Erikson sees adolescence as a time for debating, very intensely, what it means 'to be or not to be' is also unsurprising. The anxiety arising from this debate is one reason why you can have such wonderfully existentialist conversations with adolescents, but it is also why they write so much poetry about death and disaster, and sex and love. It is also why incidences of the onset of anorexia and abusive steroid use, along with other risky behaviours from very fast car- and bike-driving to unsafe sex, abound at this age. This identity formation, as we have already said, is inextricably intertwined with the biological changes of puberty. The high rate of suicide among 16–19-year-old young men, for instance has been associated strongly with unresolved fears concerning gender identity.

Tutors have a responsibility to help tutees negotiate their way through this stage effectively, but we cannot solve everybody's problems, nor make the negotiation of the developmental phase successful for all pupils, all of the time!

This is because, as Erikson suggests, an adolescent is not a *tabula rasa* (blank sheet). He or she brings to adolescence certain psychological assets and also certain liabilities arising from their previous negotiations of Life Stages

Table 6.1: Erikson's eight life stages

	Task	Meaning	Significant figure
Stage 1 (0–1)	Basic trust versus mistrust	Can I get and give in return?	Mother or mother figure/primary carer
Stage 2 (1–3)	Autonomy versus shame and doubt	Can I hold on and let go?	Parents
Stage 3 (3–6)	Initiative versus guilt	Can I make (going (after)? Can I make like (playing)?	Basic family
Stage 4 (7–12)	Industry versus inferiority	Can I make things (completing) and make things together?	Neighbourhood and school
Stage 5 (12–18)	Identity versus role confusion	To be or not to be?/ To share being oneself	Peer group, leadership models
Stage 6 (20s)	Intimacy versus isolation	To lose and find oneself in another	Partnerships in friendship, sex, competition and co-operation
Stage 7 (late 20s–50s)	Generativity versus stagnation	To make exist, to take care of	Divided labour and shared household
Stage 8 (50s and beyond)	Ego integrity versus despair	To be through having been; to face not being	Humankind, my kind

1–3 (see Table 6.1). Perhaps one way to look at the tutor's role then, psychologically, is to see it in terms of encouraging and strengthening the former, and counteracting and diminishing the effects of the latter – no more, but certainly no less.

The psychological *assets* a child may bring to adolescence include:

- A sense of knowing what it means to be 'listened to', to feel one's views are being taken seriously (in little things, not only in big ones)
- A sense of not being pressurized to 'perform'. One writer puts it like this: 'A child needs to know that there is no such thing as failure – only unreal expectations.'

The psychological *liabilities* a child may bring to adolescence include:

- Fear of being 'nobody' with no experience of love, no sense of one's own substance, and no sense of one's own value.
- Feelings of neurotic rather than 'true' guilt, which can develop through an individual receiving bad training (or no training) in values.
- Fear of not being in the mainstream, for example being an introvert in a very extroverted society. Failure to handle this sort of fear can lead to an individual finding it hard to make friends, and sometimes to being bullied.
- Fear of being unable to cope with the world: the world of 'them', of sex, of stress, of fighting for a job.

Failure to cope with any or all of these negative liabilities can lead an individual either to turn in on themselves or to become over-aggressive.

SOCIO-CULTURAL FACTORS

How far a pastoral tutor is, or should be expected to be, a role model, counsellor, PSE teacher, or even provider of a substitute 'family' structure, is viewed differently by different schools and in different cultures. What is crucial, however, is that you learn for yourself where to set the boundaries between these roles. Teachers are not trained counsellors, priests or social workers, but their work may at times contain elements of all three. The culture in which the school is situated also offers its own constraints for tutors.

Schools have to be aware of the socio-cultural demands of the local and national context in which they operate, as much as they are aware of the biological and psychological factors affecting their pupils. These, too, can and will affect your work as a tutor working with adolescents – for, as some have said, 'adolescence begins in biology but it ends in culture'. For instance, in Britain today:

- 25 per cent of children under 16 have experienced a divorce in the family;
- one in three marriages end in divorce;
- there are changes in family structures overall;
- working patterns have been, and still are, radically shifting;
- lifestyle patterns (e.g. living near or far away from family of origin) have been, and still are, radically shifting;
- the onset of puberty is now earlier than before;
- sexual experiences are also generally beginning earlier;
- the availability of money to the young is very different from in previous generations. This may lead to being valued not by what you are but by what you have;
- there are changing trends in use and abuse of drugs and substances;
- the power of the media, availability of videos (including pornographic ones) and the strong influence of popular music heavily affects young peoples' views of themselves;
- the role of religion is shifting continuously;

- the way young people are seen in relation to crime and punishment is shifting;
- the views of adults about how 'young people' should be are shifting;
- some would say young people in liberal Western democracies have more choice and more freedom than ever before in any society. They differ as to whether this is a good thing.[2]

Young people in the secondary stage of schooling need you to know about these constraints because they need: 'the ethical soundness, credibility and rational consistency of the society and the world around them in order to establish a stable identity and find meaning in life' (Erikson 1984, p. 21). The pastoral system in many schools aims to provide that as one element in the experience of their pupils. The tutor is asked to contribute to the successful accomplishment of that task.

DEALING WITH BOUNDARY ISSUES

Even supposing there was all the time in the world to do the job of a pastoral tutor, we have all, at one time or another, found ourselves severely pressurized by pastoral work and unsure that we have the skills to deal with it. Teachers are not, after all, given much initial teacher training for this part of their role. Basically though, good tutors, like all other teachers, need relevant kinds of knowledge, understanding and skills to do their job well. The trouble is that it is never very clear how, when or from whom we are going to be able to get these. Take, for instance the problems of knowing that a young man on his first work experience has encountered racial abuse at work and doesn't know how to handle it other than by physically lashing out at his employer. Or the problems of knowing that a young woman is in deep distress (which she won't tell you about for fear of peer group recriminations), which turns out to be the result of having been pressurized by an older boy into a sexual relationship she does not know how to handle. In each case, an elementary knowledge of the law as it affects young people's employment, or sexuality, or race relations, is fairly essential. But what one also needs is skill in handling *boundary issues,* i.e. determining whether this problem is one you can or should be dealing with, and then determining either how to deal with it yourself or who to refer it on to.

Tutors often acquire what amounts to a pastoral 'caseload' and can then be stuck with enormous problems of time management and prioritization. Their skills lie in not ducking but in dealing effectively with this load, whilst still knowing that their prime role is that of a classroom teacher.

The prime skills for managing this load involve good basic administration skills, but also, sometimes, good basic *counselling skills.* Good counsellors set boundaries on when, where and for how long they will listen, but they also undertake to listen, within those boundaries, attentively and genuinely to that person as a person (not just as pupil x who is 'always in trouble' or pupil y who is 'good at maths', etc.).

One such strategy involves saying to a young person, when they come to you for help (and particularly if you are very rushed): 'On a scale of 0 to 10 how serious is the problem now?' It may sound facile, but usually that person will immediately say: '4, or 7 or, oh, it's only a 1 at the moment.' This really helps you to decide whether or not you need to put other issues 'on hold' while you deal this particular pastoral problem. It also enables you, as things develop, to say casually at the start of each tutor period to that person, 'What point of the scale are we on, today then, Donna/Ben?' Apart from anything else, this keeps you in touch with both the problem and the young person's abilities to solve it for themselves. We have to bear in mind that adolescents need (with apologies to Vygotsky) *emotional* 'scaffolding' to learn how to manage their own affective development. They also need you to know, for their own sake, when to remove some or all of that 'scaffolding' in order for them to become adult. Creating a collusive co-dependence that suggests you will solve all their problems is not the way to do this. Refusing to help them at all or not acknowledging that dealing with emotional 'stuff' is hard, is counter-productive. Adolescents need to learn, as all of us have to, to take responsibility for their own actions. They have to learn to find solutions to emotional and other difficulties through their own reason, their own friendship groups and their own developing relationships with adult teachers, who up until this stage in their development have largely been seen simply as 'authority'. They need to start to make the transition between teacher as 'parent figure' and teacher as potentially equal status adult. This one transition provides, probably, at least half the work of the pastoral tutor working with this age group. We may act as better role models, for young people, of this adult attitude to life if we gently but firmly indicate the paths available to them to sort their own issues out, rather than always solving their problems for them.

It is tempting, perhaps, to argue that dealing with an individual's psychological, social and emotional developmental problems is irrelevant to our primary teaching task, which, on the surface, is merely to do with their cognitive development. However, as the psychologist Arthur Maslow pointed out, it may be, on the contrary, that until those primary needs are met, significant cognitive development is impossible. Many schools implicitly recognize this by providing pre-school breakfasts for children, or just by recognizing that in times of deep emotional distress, some of the important things a young person needs to encounter are, as Maslow suggested when he produced his 'pyramid of needs', routine, trust and acceptance, the esteem and respect of others, being part of a group, and protection from potentially dangerous objects or situations (Maslow 1984). An adolescent bereaved, for instance, will certainly need these aspects of schooling to be there as he or she comes to terms with grief and loss.

Tutors have, legally, to adhere to rules in many aspects of their practice. These govern their ability to promise confidentiality to a pupil and their responsibility for knowing where, in relationships between pupil, tutor, school hierarchy, family and the local community, they are qualified, and therefore allowed, to intervene. This takes time to learn, but is at the basic competence level of tutoring. What is far more difficult is learning how and when it is important to down 'teacher-as-educator' tools and pick up 'teacher-as-pastoral-carer' ones.

In summary, however, the golden rules for tutoring seem to be:

- Administrate efficiently and deal with problems as promptly as you can.
- Listen carefully – and genuinely. Take time to do so.
- Set clear boundaries to help the tutees know what they have responsibility for and what you have responsibility for in each situation.
- Know who to refer particular problems to.
- Never attempt to take a pupil's 'side' in a dispute without first checking:

  (a) that their side of the story fits with that of others involved in it (particularly important when there are disciplinary conflicts between staff and pupils);
  (b) which other staff should, or already do, know about the problem (sometimes pupils start to tell several staff the same problem and end up getting everyone running round after them!);
  (c) what viable possibilities there are for pupils to solve the problem themselves, with or without emotional 'scaffolding'.

CONCLUSION

As other chapters in this book point out, what we are doing, in all aspects of schooling, including tutoring, involves providing a good deal of implicit and explicit values education alongside the delivery of the formal curriculum. When we undertake, in maintained schools, the management of pastoral problems, we need to be very clear about what this means for us, both as individual teachers and as individuals collectively responsible to parents for the safe keeping of their children. Some schools see the tutoring role as merely instrumental, i.e. picking up problems as they arise and responding pragmatically to them. The dangers of this approach are, of course, that a lot of problems go unnoticed. There may also be, on this reading of the role of the tutor, little or no attempt by the school to deliver consistent values education within the tutor group. Given our responsibilities under the 1988 Education Reform Act for the pupils' spiritual moral, cultural and social development, it is becoming less and less usual for tutor groups to function in this way. Many schools now see the tutor group as a space for encouraging not only cognitive and affective development, but also spiritual and moral development. This may be done in a variety of ways, from explicit collective worship to 'thought for the day'-type explorations of current events and issues of general human concern. Either way, it is a clear attempt to influence pupils' values. This is new territory for many teachers, and many feel reluctant, and certainly ill-equipped, to engage in such activity. It is worth noting, however, that while both the definitions and the practical outworking of a moral and spiritual, or indeed a citizenship education in maintained schools has yet to be fully formalized, discussion about it is very much alive and important within the educational community. Trainee teachers would be wise to engage with the debate in their initial teacher training, since there may be less time to do so once they are full-time teachers.

Perhaps we can best regard different forms of pastoral tutoring as the attempt to find a 'best fit' solution to the need for schools, located in and representing very diverse cultures, to support their pupils through a crucial, if sometimes difficult phase of their psychological, emotional and cognitive development. This, done well, is part of the whole complex process by which schooling should enable young people to enter the increasingly complex world of adult community with as many cognitive and affective strengths, and as few liabilities, as possible.

NOTES

1. Adolescence, late 1990s-style, is subject to some pretty difficult and possibly unique pressures, but that doesn't mean it might not also be much the same thing as it always was. If you read this quote and try to date it you may get a glimpse of what I mean:

> The young are in character prone to desire and ready to carry any desire they may form into action. Of bodily desires it is the sexual to which they are most disposed to give way, and in regard to sexual desire they exercise no self-restraint. They are changeful too and fickle in their desires, which are as transitory as they are vehement; for their wishes are keen without being permanent, like a sick man is prone to fits of hunger and thirst.
>
> . . . if the young commit a fault, it is always on the side of excess and exaggeration for they carry everything too far, whether it be love or hatred or anything else. They regard themselves as omniscient and are positive in their assertion; this is, in fact, the reason for their carrying everything too far.

The date? Well you might be able to tell that it's not recent from the language, but would you have guessed it was in fact written by Aristotle, 2,300 years ago?

2. In her fascinating, though now rather dated and sometimes criticized study of adolescence in Samoa, *Coming of Age in Samoa*, the anthropologist Margaret Mead claimed to find little evidence of the existence of huge emotional disturbances which are sometimes regarded in our own culture as an inevitable (and incurably awful!) side-effect of adolescence. But she did still see socio-cultural factors as important. Mead put the apparent absence of emotional stress in adolescence in Samoan culture at that time down to the general casualness of Samoan society and its unhurried pace, to the looseness of its family and other interpersonal bonds, to the absence of economic, social or other crises; and, to a considerable extent, to the absence of a necessity for individual choice – vocationally, socially or morally.

Such studies highlight the importance for us, as teachers, of being aware of the pressures our own society is making on its young people today. For instance, is adolescence becoming more stressful because of the increasing diversity and complexity of society today? To take one small example. Sitting down to help a Year 12 pupil look through the UCAS handbook recently brought home to me the vast proliferation of courses (and universities!) to which she could go at 18, or at 21, or, indeed, at 41 or 81! Making career choices against such a background is very different from making them 20, let alone 40 or 50 years ago! The choice is affected by everything from economics, through gender to politics and family structures. To ignore all these factors would not make us good secondary school teachers, let alone good pastoral tutors.

Chapter 7

Special Educational Needs: Current Concerns, Future Opportunities

MARTYN ROUSE

SPECIAL EDUCATIONAL NEEDS: A BRIEF OVERVIEW

This chapter will consider some of the issues that teachers and schools have to face as they attempt to educate all students, in particular those who are thought to have special educational needs (SEN). The chapter will provide a brief overview of key developments in the field of SEN and will examine some of the assumptions that underpin recent thinking in this area. It will conclude by considering the responsibilities and opportunities that all teachers share in maximizing the learning of all children and young people in the light of these recent developments.

The history of special education in the United Kingdom can be traced back more than 200 years to a time when the first special schools were founded for the deaf and the blind. Much of the impetus for these early developments in the education of disabled children was rooted in charity. In 1870, the introduction of compulsory schooling brought into schools many children who previously did not receive an education, because it was believed they would not benefit from such an investment of time and money. Furthermore, the Industrial Revolution saw the mass relocation of populations from rural to urban communities and an associated decline in natural support systems such as extended families and traditional crafts for disabled people. In response to the concerns that this raised, separate special schools and institutions were created to cater for those children who were considered unsuitable for normal schooling and who were seen as so demanding of their families that they might undermine economic efficiency.

Associated with the growth of special education was the belief that disabled people, particularly those with learning difficulties or mental health problems, needed to be cared for, and that this could best be done by segregating them into asylums located away from populous areas. The reasons why this solution was adopted are complex. They result from a combination of factors, including a humanitarian concern for those less fortunate than the majority, and the growing need for social control. The influence of eugenic thinking was also apparent. It suggested that such people should be segregated, controlled and not allowed to have children for fear of contaminating the gene pool. Thus, the institutionalization of disabled people has its origins in *protection*; the protection of the community of 'normal' people from the disabled through segregated forms of provision, and the protection of disabled people from themselves through humanitarian care. Segregated special schools were often founded upon the same principles of protection and care.

During the twentieth century, special education developed as a separate but parallel system with its own career structures and teaching approaches. Over time, new eligible categories of handicap were established, and at the time of the 1944 Education Act, ten categories of handicap were recognized. In spite of this growth in special provision, still not all children were entitled to education. Those with severe learning difficulties were the responsibility of health authorities and were placed in long-stay hospitals or junior training centres, rather than schools.

In England and Wales the 1970 Education Act made local education authorities (LEAs) responsible for the education of *all* children, regardless of the severity of their disability. This legislation recognized the right of all children to education and required LEAs to provide such schooling. What this meant in practice was that the existing junior training centres became ESN(S) schools serving what were then called educationally sub-normal (severe) pupils. New teaching approaches developed in many of these schools and gradually it became accepted that no child was ineducable. The 1970s were a time of rapid growth in the field of special education.

Much of this progress came about as a result of parental pressure. Parents and carers have played a major role in the struggle to establish and maintain these hard-won rights for their children to receive an appropriate education. Often this struggle was organized through the numerous voluntary societies, charities and pressure groups that have been instrumental in many positive developments in special education. Unfortunately, the field has been, and still is, vulnerable to promises of 'miracle cures'. The history of special education is littered with initiatives that promised much but delivered little.

Wedell (1990) has pointed out that few areas of education have seen such major developments during the past twenty years as special needs education. Much of the legislation for special education in England and Wales (e.g. the Education Acts of 1970 and 1981) could be described as enabling, permissive and progressive. The Education Act of 1970 provided access to education for children with the most severe disabilities. The Warnock Report (DES 1978), which was the basis of the 1981 Act, reflected a non-categorical, altruistic, and benevolent view of special education. The Report introduced the concept of 'special educational need'. It broadened and loosened definitions, suggesting that as many as 20 per cent of children could have a learning difficulty at some stage of their school careers. Parents were seen as playing a central role in the identification, assessment and education of their children alongside benign caring professionals. During the 1970s and 1980s, such thinking was the basis of developments in policy and practice in many schools and LEAs. It led to a reconceptualization of the special needs task based upon the following principles which are still influential today:

- *Interactive nature of difficulty*: special educational needs result from a complex interaction of factors, only some of which exist within the child. Other factors are found in the learning environment in which the child is educated. Acknowledging the importance of the context in which learning occurs has led to what is sometimes called an 'ecological perspective' which rejects the so-called 'medical model'. Interactive explanations recognize that a child might have a learning difficulty in one classroom but not in another. At their heart is the belief that teachers make a difference to how well, or badly, children learn.
- *Non-categorical nature of disability*: special needs are relative and context-specific. It is therefore impossible to draw a clear line between the so-called handicapped and non-handicapped. Furthermore the use of categorical labels, which might be useful in securing resources, often led to unhelpful stereotyping and lower expectations. Much of the provision that currently exists, together with many people's attitudes, remains based upon categorical assumptions of disability. The field has found it difficult to leave 'labels' behind.
- *Common aims*: the aims of education are the same for all children, although the means may be different, as might the extent to which the aims are achieved.
- *Inclusion*: children have the right to be educated alongside their peers as long as their needs can be met. Additional support and different approaches to school structures and teaching may be required if this is to be achieved. Inclusive schools set out to educate all children, regardless of disability and diversity. They see diversity as a resource for learning rather than as inevitably leading to problems.
- *Positive discrimination*: some children might need additional help and support if they are to learn successfully in school. The current law aims to protect their rights by issuing a 'statement of special educational need', a legal document detailing the form of provision and additional support required. However, it must not be assumed that additional help is always required, nor that such help necessarily leads to positive benefits for the child. Indeed there are many examples of inappropriate help harming children's learning, particularly when unskilled adult intervention separates the child from the curriculum.

Evidence suggests that progress was made in implementing new policies and practice based upon these principles (Wedell *et al.* 1987). Spending on special education increased during the 1980s, LEAs appointed new advisory teams and there was a series of new teacher and school development initiatives designed to promote whole-school policies for meeting special needs.

In spite of these developments, problems in the field of special educational needs remain. It is possible to be critical of the consequences of the enabling and permissive special education policies that were so influential during the past twenty years. The lack of a clear framework and the absence of agreed definitions of what constitutes a special educational need led to wide variation in practice both between and within LEAs. The special needs debate became dominated by questions about resources: which children are entitled to receive additional help? At a time when funding was limited, there was pressure to relocate resources from certain existing groups to new or redefined kinds of special need.

As previously mentioned, Warnock suggested that as many as 20 per cent of children might have a special difficulty of some kind at some stage of their school lives. Of these children, the majority (18 per cent) would not require additional support. Under the current arrangements, schools are urged to follow a standard procedure for the assessment of a pupil's special educational needs prior to asking for a formal statutory assessment leading to a 'statement'; this staged process is explained in the *Code of Practice on the Identification of Special Educational Needs* (DFE 1994). Statements are made for those pupils whose needs are such that extra resources are considered necessary to enable them to learn effectively. A statement is central to securing adequate educational provision for children who will require specialized help. An unintended consequence of this, however, has been that schools use the statementing process as the means through which they can secure additional resources from the local educational authority. The resulting bureaucracy has not served children or schools well, because it consumes too much time and professional effort that could be focused on improving teaching and learning.

It was thought back in the early 1980s that around 2 per cent of children would require the protection of a statement of special educational need. Coincidentally, this was, overall, the same percentage that was being educated in special schools. However, in some LEAs this figure was as low as 0.6 per cent, but in others it was as high as 6 per cent. These differences could not be explained by the relative incidence of disability in various regions; rather they were a result of the historic patterns of provision or of differences in interpretation of the government's guidelines by the LEAs. There was also confusion about the rights of the remaining 18 per cent of Warnock's '20 per cent', the majority of whom were, and always had been, in mainstream schools. In addition, special schools were under increasing scrutiny to justify their additional costs. These, and other problems facing special education, were highlighted by two reports commissioned by government and carried out by the Audit Commission (1992a, 1992b). In response to these concerns the government introduced new legislation in 1993 which led to the *Code of Practice on the Identification and Assessment of Special Educational Needs* in 1994.

In spite of the difficulties outlined above, the 1980s was a period during which many people assumed that special education provision would continue to grow because of the permissive policy framework. Although the special needs task in many schools has been complicated in recent years by a number of changes that have challenged traditional thinking about the nature of disability and learning difficulty, few people anticipated that the political and educational climate would change so radically that it would threaten the assumptions upon which existing practice and provision was based.

Special education, just like the rest of education, was about to feel the consequences of a shift from legislation and policies based upon the principles of equity, social progress, altruism and benign professionalism to new legislation, the Education Reform Act 1988, underpinned by the principles of academic excellence, choice, competition and parental self-interest. A spirit of 'educational Darwinism' became apparent in which only the fittest students, teachers and schools would survive. In a climate based upon the principles of the market, students with special educational needs were to become particularly vulnerable.

The Education Reform Act was to have a radical impact upon the education of children with special needs, although they were not mentioned in any of the original documentation. In particular, the National Curriculum and its associated systems of assessment would change the educational landscape and challenge the thinking of many parents and professionals about whether the educational aims for all children were, or could be, the same. Although the National Curriculum has been a challenge for all teachers of children with special educational needs, it is the impact of the curriculum for the statemented group in particular (recently estimated as 3 per cent and rising) which has been most difficult (McLaughlin and Tilstone 1999).

The rapid changes of the last ten years or so have caused turmoil in the field of special educational needs. In spite of, or maybe because of, these changes, there have been many innovative developments that might provide the impetus for improvements in future practice. There is a series of issues such as assessment, the relationship between teaching and learning, inclusion and the future of segregated special forms of provision, that face schools as they attempt to make sense of the special needs task in the context of recent reforms. Each of these will be considered below.

ASSESSMENT

Assessment has played a pivotal role in the development of policies and practice in special education. Traditionally, this task was directed towards categorizing and segregating children with disabilities and learning difficulties in order to find those children who would not benefit from mainstream schooling. Various screening and identification procedures were developed for this purpose so that problems could be named and diagnosed and appropriate placement and provision made. In addition, professionals have employed a variety of methods for the assessment of children in order to plan appropriate interventions for them. It could be argued that approaches to assessment which saw abilities as fixed inevitably had negative consequences for children, by labelling them inappropriately and by lowering teachers' expectations.

The methods of assessment used at any particular time are a reflection of a number of factors, including the prevailing perspectives on the nature of special needs as well as the various political purposes for assessment. As a result, over time, a number of major approaches to assessment in special needs have emerged. These are:

- analysis of the learner;
- analysis of the learning task;
- analysis of the learning environment;
- the analysis of learning outcomes.

There was widespread dissatisfaction with the first two of these approaches to assessment, and with the consequences of such approaches. These concerns coincided with the growing recognition that contextual factors, such as the quality of teaching and the curriculum, have a major impact on learning. Thus, it was argued that learning difficulties could only be understood in the context in which they occurred. Such interactive, or ecological, explanations became an essential feature of the concept of special educational needs that emerged from the Warnock enquiry (DES 1978) mentioned above. This interactionist view suggests that since the child's learning takes place in particular contexts, assessment should not simply take no account of that context and its influence on the child. More appropriate methods adopt an 'ecological perspective' which recognizes features of the learning context such as the curriculum, the teaching, the organization of the classroom and other school variables as essential factors that influence learning. These ideas influenced the enactment of the 1981 Education Act and subsequent changes in the concept of special education, in which the thinking about discrete categories of 'handicap' began to be replaced by the idea of a continuum of 'special educational needs' (SEN).

Analysing the learning environment as an approach to assessment of special needs, does not prescribe *particular* forms for assessment. However, it does recognize the importance of teachers in the assessment process and it values the information that teachers have about their students. Proponents of this view of assessment also stress the need for students to play an active role in their own assessment, through negotiation and collaboration.

Therefore teachers have to make assessment-based decisions. Such decisions have the capacity to improve teaching and learning as a whole, and in particular provide for the learning needs of children who are experiencing difficulties. One way in which teachers can provide for the needs of their pupils is to use assessment to plan their teaching activity. The work of Susan Hart (1996) is significant here. She urges teachers to scrutinize the evidence they collect about children's responses and to use innovative thinking to help interpret what is happening. By seeking alternative explanations for difficulty, teachers can gain valuable insights that can be used to help learners who may be finding learning hard. In such ways, it can be argued that assessment has evolved from being a separate entity in special education, the main purpose of which was for selection and placement, to a growing recognition of the central role of teacher assessment in improving teaching and learning. The power of formative (i.e. *informative*) assessment to improve learning in the classroom is increasingly accepted. To be effective, feedback needs to be explicit, specific and rapid (Black 1996).

Summative assessment in the National Curriculum combines teacher assessment and national, externally prescribed tests and tasks (Standard Assessment Tasks or Tests: SATs). Statutorily prescribed SATs are administered in the final year of a Key Stage and methods of assessment vary depending on the subject and the Key Stage. The impact of these approaches has radically affected the ways in which teachers view the assessment task (Rouse and Agbenu 1998). The work of Lewis (1995, 1996) suggests that the following issues apply to children with special educational needs:

- the process of combining data to arrive at a standard test and task level has masked attainments, especially for children with learning difficulties, for whom small gains and/or uneven development need to be acknowledged;
- the aggregated results of the SATs published in league tables in the national press emphasize the performance of schools with the highest attainments, implying that other schools are failing. Some schools are reluctant, therefore, either to admit children with special educational needs or to enter them for SATs in case they depress the scores;
- from Key Stage 2 onwards, testing in mainstream and special schools is often undertaken under formal examination conditions which are unfamiliar to children with special educational needs, causing anxiety and contributing to poor performance.

Although difficulties remain in developing a national system of assessment that will meaningfully include all children and enable them to demonstrate their learning, there is little doubt that the current preoccupation with standards has raised awareness in the profession. It has also has introduced a sense of urgency into the task of raising the levels of achievement of those children who find learning difficult.

CLASSROOM FACTORS: TEACHING APPROACHES

In a recent research project investigating the practice of nearly 300 secondary teachers working in inclusive schools, Florian and Rouse (1999) found that many teachers were able to identify, describe and use particular teaching strategies and approaches that successfully include all learners. These strategies include peer tutoring, co-teaching, role playing, co-operative learning, and 'jigsawing'. The schools that took part in this investigation provide opportunities for teachers to learn about the use of such strategies in their own classrooms and encourage teachers to extend their range of teaching approaches.

In addition to the strategies mentioned above, there are other features that seem to characterize classrooms where children's learning needs are most effectively met. A good example concerns the use of praise. When appropriately used, perhaps in private, as part of the feedback process, praise can be a powerful means of improving self-esteem which is an essential component of successful learning.

Teachers who are effective in meeting children's special needs have high, but realistic, academic and behaviour expectations of the children they teach. They accept that all pupils can learn, but that some children may need alternative explanations and examples. In particular, it seems important for teachers to make connections between what is being learned and what is already known and has been experienced. One way of doing this is to begin each session by explaining the aims of the lesson to the pupils and linking it to previous learning.

Active learning plays an important part in successful classrooms. The experiences that are organized for the children should be as authentic as possible. Many children who find abstract classroom learning difficult have few problems learning out of school.

Grouping and organizational strategies should be appropriate for the activity that is taking place. For example, if it is necessary to give instructions, it is better to address the whole class and to ensure that they can all see and hear the teacher. Similarly, children should only work in groups when they are working on a collaborative task. Properly structured collaborative group work has been demonstrated to be one of the most effective ways of meeting a wide range of learning needs within the classroom because it utilizes other children, one of the major resources for learning in the classroom.

INCLUSION

Inclusive education refers to a philosophy and practice of education based on the following principles:

* All children have the right to learn and play together.
* Children should not be devalued or discriminated against by being excluded or sent away because of their disability or learning difficulty.
* There are no legitimate academic reasons to separate children for the duration of their schooling.
* They belong together rather than need to be protected from one another.

Despite the difficulties associated with the implementation of inclusive education policies, there is a great deal of philosophical agreement about the rights of children with special educational needs to equal educational opportunity. The concept of inclusion is a central theme in the government's education policies. The extent to which the legislative process currently under way will help to ensure that pupils with special educational needs are justly included in the new education reform proposals is unclear. However, the acknowledgement that children with special educational needs are to be included in the drive for higher standards is a challenging and an exciting development, though there are many problems to overcome.

Current government policy as outlined in the *Special Educational Needs: A Programme for Action* (DfEE 1998) adopts a policy of increased inclusion but within a framework of special education. It clearly advocates a continuation of the highly individualized approach for children with complex needs. However, other policy revisions aim to 'develop an education system in which specialist provision is seen as an integral part of overall provision' (*ibid.*, p. 44). Whether the actual policies which evolve from this process will help facilitate better educational opportunity for *all* remains to be seen. What is certain is that over a period of 30 years, innovative teachers have been able to demonstrate that all pupils can learn, despite policies which excluded certain children from mainstream schools. Their contribution to the development of educational methods with applicability to *all learners* represented a significant advance in extending the right to education for all. Today, the human rights agenda which demands the adoption of inclusive education policies requires the same level of innovation from all professionals to demonstrate that all children can learn together.

Much of the research on inclusive classrooms has focused on primary schools and the difficulties associated with teacher resistance to inclusion or lack of knowledge about appropriate teaching approaches. It is therefore interesting to note that those schools that have made the commitment to support teachers in the development of their skills report fewer difficulties in implementation of inclusive practices which work to the benefit of all children.

FUTURE OF SPECIAL SCHOOLS

Developments in inclusion have implications for the future role of special schools. One current view is that special schools could become regional resource centres to support developments in mainstream schools. This suggestion is however, problematic. Many of the approaches developed in special schools, such as one-to-one teaching and daily monitoring of progress, are not mainstream-friendly and do not easily relocate from special to mainstream settings. In addition, many teachers who work in special schools have little experience of mainstream settings or of working with and through other adults as curriculum consultants. One area of expertise that special schools have developed is multi-professional collaboration. There is much that mainstream schools could learn in this regard.

Special schools are increasingly being judged against many of the same criteria that apply to mainstream schools. Questions about value for time and money are relevant here because of the significantly greater costs in educating a child in a special rather than a mainstream school.

CONCLUSION

The core debate in the area of special educational needs has been dominated in recent years by two main concerns. The first relates to *resources*; who should receive them and how should the distribution of any additional resources be monitored. The second has been about *location; special or mainstream*. These debates are likely to continue, but hopefully the future will see more professional energy being concentrated on the fundamental issue of how children learn best. The task is not to identify more children with special educational needs, but to create classrooms and schools which do not produce learning difficulties as a consequence of the teaching approaches used. One thing is clear; teachers make a difference, and good teaching is the key to improving children's learning and to reducing the number of children who have special educational needs. This is the challenge for *all* teachers, not only those who have chosen to make their careers in special needs work.

Chapter 8

Equal Opportunities and Educational Performance: Gender, Race and Class

MADELEINE ARNOT

It is one of the paradoxes of the 1988 Education Reform Act that, even though it was assumed that 'the pursuit of egalitarianism is now over' (Kenneth Baker, then Secretary of State for Education), the effect of the legislation has been to promote greater public concern about the unequal performance of different groups of children in the school system and onwards. Social inequalities now receive considerable public exposure from the publication of school performance tables, the breakdown of National Test results (SATs) into gender categories and, for example, the publication of Ofsted reviews such as that by Gillborn and Gipps (1996) on the achievement of ethnic minority pupils, and Arnot *et al.* (1998) on recent research on gender and educational performance.

Although the level of support offered to schools from LEA advisers and specialist teachers on equal opportunities, financial assistance and networking between schools, has declined in many areas of the country in the last fifteen years (Arnot *et al.* 1996), there were signs in 1995 of a 'third wave' of interest in gender equality issues, particularly in the rural shires. The increased attention given to differences in academic performance in the standardized tests and in the GCSE results, especially by Ofsted inspectors, highlighted for schools the importance of monitoring and reducing gender inequalities in outcomes (*ibid.*). The new debate about girls' and boys' schooling is therefore directly related to issues of standards and performance rather than to the more general concerns of gender equality and social justice (Arnot *et al.* 1999).

In contrast, the issue of ethnicity has had a far more chequered career in the last decade. In 1985, the Swann Committee (1985) in its investigation of the achievement levels of ethnic minority children, endorsed the concept of multiculturalism (which it called *Education for All*). Nevertheless, the Education Reform Act 1988 made only passing references to the need for schools to promote cultural diversity within existing programmes of study and as part of one of the cross-curricular 'dimensions' identified by the National Curriculum

Council. No official guidance was published. By the 1990s, the use of targeted funding through what used to be known as Section 11 grants (since April 1999 renamed the Ethnic Minority Achievement Grant (EMAG)) was tightly focused upon helping students with difficulties in English. Thus, little support was offered (either financial or advisory) on how to tackle racism within schooling. Sociological research continued, nevertheless, to point to racial harassment and race attacks in schools and communities, to experiences of black pupils in secondary schools which negatively affected their identities as learners, and to their perceptions about how their communities were regarded by white pupils (see Gillborn 1995; Troyna and Hatcher 1992; Connolly 1998; Wright *et al.* 1998).

Support for multicultural education and initiatives to combat racism in education regained political currency again in 1998 after the Gillborn and Gipps (1996) review *Recent Research on the Achievements of Ethnic Minority Pupils* documented the extensive differences in achievement between ethnic groups in a range of different localities. Although schools collect their own ethnic data, no national statistics are available. LEA data, however, indicate the continuing inequalities in achievement between white and ethnic minority communities, and the alarmingly high rate of expulsion of some black children. Black African Caribbean pupils have been found to be between three and six times more likely to be excluded from schools, and the proportion of black boys has been found to be over-represented by a factor of up to eight (*ibid.*). Government concern about such forms of institutional racism in schools was raised in a very direct fashion by the report of Sir William McPherson (1999) on the murder of Stephen Lawrence. This report drew the government's and the public's attention to the importance of schools promoting racial tolerance through multiculturalism and developing new strategies to combat racism. These renewed concerns are directly linked to the promotion of citizenship education for all pupils.

Gillborn and Gipps' review of research also revealed the extent to which ethnic minority communities such as the Bangladeshi community in the East End of London were *improving* their educational qualifications. Furthermore, statistics and case studies suggest that certain patterns of positive achievement (rather than failure) by particular groups of ethnic minority pupils, e.g. Indian pupils, and by ethnic minority girls, e.g. African–Caribbean and Muslim girls, should be recognized, if black pupils are not to continue to be collectively stigmatized as 'a problem' and as failures. Teachers had been found to have unrealistically low expectations of African–Caribbean pupils in particular, and to find explanations for the low academic achievement of certain black pupils by stereotyping their communities and their homes. More recognition is now needed of the value which the great majority of ethnic minority communities place on schooling (Basit 1997; Mirza 1992) and the importance of working collaboratively with such communities (e.g. Bastiani 1997).

THE BOYS' ACHIEVEMENT DEBATE

The interest in gender and race issues often comes together in discussions about boys' educational experiences. The relatively low academic performance of male pupils, especially of both black and white working-class boys, has become a matter of great concern for schools attempting to improve their literacy levels and overall performance. The press has called the relative underachievement of boys a 'crisis in masculinity'. Various chapters in the Epstein *et al.* collection *Failing Boys?* (1998) suggest how and why this debate has developed in the 1990s in the UK (in much the same way as it has developed in Australia – see Gilbert and Gillborn 1998). Two key gender gaps in performance were identified by the recent Ofsted review (Arnot *et al.* 1998): firstly the literacy gap, and secondly the different pattern of male and female success in achieving five or more higher grade GCSEs. The gap between boys and girls in terms of literacy is already established by the age of 7 and, as recent evidence shows, remains sizeable as pupils progress through schooling. Boys also lag behind girls in their performance in modern foreign languages. This difference in male and female performance in English is especially significant because not only have girls kept their advantage in such conventionally 'female' subjects but they have, with the support of teachers and schools, substantially reduced boys' traditional advantage in terms of entry into, and performance in, 'male' subjects such as Mathematics, Chemistry, and Physics (Arnot *et al.* 1996 and 1998; Kenway and Willis 1998).

By the mid-1990s, only 80 boys compared to every 100 girls were achieving five higher grade GCSEs, compared with over 90 boys in the mid-1970s. This pattern has since remained relatively stable. To some extent this comparatively slow progress of boys in improving their qualifications is associated with the increase in numbers of pupils entering for GCSE – especially after the introduction of the National Curriculum and the changed patterns of subject entry which followed. Boys and girls are now expected to succeed in subjects which traditionally they avoided. Many other theories have been put forward to explain why boys have failed to match the substantial improvement in girls' performance. Attention has, for example, been focused on boys' 'laddish' culture, which represents schooling – and especially 'feminized' subjects such as English and literacy – as 'not cool'. Commentators also point to the collapse of traditional male transitions from school to work because of the decline in manufacturing industry and the associated loss of traditional male apprenticeships. These cultural and economic factors suggest that many boys, who traditionally used to 'pick up' in terms of academic achievement in secondary schools, may have lost motivation and, especially by Years 8 and 9, have, in some cases, become disaffected from schooling.

The levels of disaffection amongst boys has been noted by researchers in a range of different studies (see Arnot *et al.* 1998 and MacDonald *et al.* 1999). The evidence is interesting but remains inconclusive. Far more attention, however, has been paid to boys' learning preferences and the reasons why boys report lower levels of enjoyment at school. There is interest in whether boys and girls prefer different subjects, and whether they respond differently to, for example, coursework/project work, extended writing, factual teaching, also whether they are motivated differently in relation to the same subject. Research has also encouraged an interest in whether boys and girls are equally comfortable with different styles of assessment: for example, is their performance affected by the choice of items for assessment, terminal examinations, multiple choice versus course work, etc? The Ofsted review on gender research (Arnot *et al.* 1998) offered the following summary of research findings:

- Girls are more attentive in class and more willing to learn. They do better on sustained tasks that are open-ended, process-based, relate to realistic situations and require thinking for oneself. Girls may over-rate the difficulty of particular subjects. Girls find timed end-of-course examinations less congenial. Teachers believe that course work favours girls, but other factors (including syllabus selection) may be more important.
- Boys show greater adaptability to traditional approaches which require memorizing abstract, unambiguous facts which have to be acquired quickly. They are more willing to sacrifice deep understanding for correct answers achieved at speed. Boys do better on multiple-choice papers, whatever the subject.

Research on teaching and learning differences between girls and boys has been identified as an important area for raising teacher awareness, encouraging the view that gender blindness (treating all pupils alike) may no longer be helpful. Investigating the similarities and differences in learning styles of boys and girls is likely to be more fruitful for identifying appropriate strategies.

At the same time, a number of other gender issues in schooling are being brought into focus. Of central importance are teachers' gender values, especially in relation to their pupils' concepts of masculinity and femininity – and the effect such values might have on pupils' learning experiences. Gender values can affect how teachers deal with, for example, male and female pupils' anxieties, their motivation to learn, their choices of subjects to study, their work experience placements and the careers advice they receive at school. In certain contexts, teachers can encourage rather than discourage male disaffection. Increasingly, researchers (cf Arnot *et al.* 1998 for references) are highlighting the following:

- Images of masculinity being legitimated by the school (through the hidden curriculum) and by teachers' interactions with boys. There is evidence from research of conflict between male and female teachers and boys, especially over overtly 'masculine' behaviour (Abraham 1995; Sewell 1997; Mac an Ghaill 1994).
- Teacher expectations about boys' abilities insofar as they affect, for example, the diagnosis of special needs (especially behavioural and emotional difficulties), learning support provision, and disciplining strategies

(expulsions, suspensions). Boys are over-represented in all these categories.

• The levels of bullying reported by pupils in the UK raise concern about teachers' responses to such incidents, especially when they involve boys. If teachers' responses are considered unfair or not sufficiently protective by pupils, then they may contribute to the lower levels of male enjoyment and engagement with schooling (Chaplain 1996).

WHICH GIRLS, WHICH BOYS?

There is a concern that the strong level of interest in boys' underachievement will ignore not just their successes, but also will fail to engage with the continuing problem of girls' lesser involvement in science. The statistics of male and female achievement reveal not only that boys do better at A level, even in female subjects such as English, but that they are far more likely to study the sciences, technology and computing at this level than girls. Despite girls' success in performing comparably in the sciences and mathematics in primary and secondary schools, boys gain a slight advantage as they progress through school, and many more boys than girls sit single-science GCSEs in Physics and Chemistry (Arnot *et al.* 1998). At A level these subjects are getting more rather than less 'masculinized', with the statistics of further and higher education also demonstrating the low proportions of girls going on after school to study science or science-related courses/degrees. Vocational courses are also still strongly sex stereotyped, with young women opting for traditional female training courses for work in the service sectors (e.g. hairdressing, beauty care, caring courses, or social studies). In this respect, they continue to make 'poor choices' in terms of post-16 training and careers, since such courses have low economic benefits. Gender stereotyping by pupils (and possibly teachers) therefore remains an ongoing issue for schools. It also remains the case that women still experience what is called a 'glass ceiling' in relation to advancement in top jobs. The Equal Opportunities Commission's (EOC) report (Rolfe 1999) argues that the careers service and school-based careers education programmes should take responsibility for promoting equal opportunities, but that this should not be interpreted solely as 'promoting entry into non-traditional areas, but focus on equal access and achievement at all levels, including in management and the professions' (p. xi).

Statistical data on achievement also suggest that the extraordinary success of girls in raising their achievement of five higher grade GCSEs may mainly apply to white girls. Data presented by Gillborn and Gipps (1996) suggest that the interconnections between gender, ethnicity and class patterns of achievement can differ substantially in different localities. Some groups of Asian boys, for example, may perform better than equivalent groups of Asian girls; whilst both African–Caribbean boys and girls might do less well than white male and female pupils (Gillborn 1997). Research has shown that gender never works in isolation: it affects and is affected by ethnic patterns of performance. Many schools recognize the need to break down performance data into ethnic sub-groups, and some local education authorities provide excellent databases which allow schools to target particular groups of underachieving pupils. Also, as indicated earlier, teachers are becoming more aware of the importance of not sustaining the notion of the 'failing black pupil', for example by recognizing patterns of improved or high levels of ethnic minority performance (see Channer 1995).

Describing social class differences is notoriously problematic and schools find it difficult to identify indices to highlight the effects of socio-economic background on pupils' performance. Often, free school meals are used as rough indicators of low income and of class status. Such indicators are unsatisfactory, but the attempt to assess the impact of class background is, nevertheless, essential since social class repeatedly has been found to be strongly associated with academic progress. The National Commission on Education (1993) reminded us that:

> Children from social classes I and II do better, on average, in examinations at 16, are more likely to stay on longer in full time education and are more likely to go to university than those in social classes III to V. There has been little change over the years in the proportion of entrants to higher education who come from working class families. (p. 8)

Evidence from a major Australian study *Who Wins at School?* (Teese *et al.* 1995) found not only that working-class girls had higher rates of failure in some subjects than other girls (for example, in English) but that working-class boys were more likely to depress the overall scores for boys in literacy, and in language more generally. Gender differences appeared narrowest where students have the greatest cultural and material advantages and sharpest where their parents were more socially disadvantaged. The lower the social status of girls, the less likely they were to take Mathematics and the more likely they were to fail when they did. Working-class boys in contrast overenrolled in Mathematics and Physics, and were more likely to play truant in classes in Literature, History or Modern Languages. Unfortunately there is no comparable study in the UK.

Whilst one should not adopt too deterministic a view about the effects of social class, it is nevertheless essential to recognize that family background and the nature of the locality can still be a critical influence on pupils' achievement. The considerable increase in the proportion of all pupils achieving higher grades in GCSE masks the serious effects of unemployment and poverty in certain parts of the UK and in particular communities – where a high proportion of single-parent families live close to the poverty line and there are few local employment opportunities for young people. Each year more than 10,000 pupils are excluded from schools as a result of disaffection and conflicts in school. The loss of traditional transitions from school to work challenges secondary schools in particular to find new ways of motivating pupils to 'stay on' and to become more flexible in their life choices. In such areas, teachers attempt a range of strategies: for example, working more closely with the community, encouraging parents to express their values and needs in relation to their children's schooling, signing up parents to contracts over homework, and becoming involved in pupil mentoring and setting homework targets. Concern about social inequality encourages schools to engage more actively with their local community.

SCHOOL EQUALITY STRATEGIES

Various agencies (e.g. the Qualifications, Curriculum and Assessment Authority, the Equal Opportunities Commission, the Secondary Heads Association, and Ofsted) have now entered the fray, with suggestions about how teachers might improve pupils' academic performance. In 1999, the Schools Standards minister, Stephen Byers, made the gender gap a matter of national concern, when he publicly encouraged each local education authority and every school to develop their own plans to tackle the differences between male and female examination performance. Improved overall school performance was seen as dependent upon such efforts. He warned that a new trend has been identified for a minority of boys who are disaffected with school, quoting figures which showed that 83 per cent of permanent exclusions are of boys and that 7,000 more boys than girls left school at 16 with no qualifications. He argued that the 'laddish anti-learning culture' which has been allowed to develop over recent years should be challenged and that we should not simply 'accept with a shrug of our shoulders that boys will be boys'. He commented:

> Failure to raise the educational achievement of boys will mean that thousands of young men will face a bleak future in which a lack of qualifications and basic skills will mean unemployment and little hope of finding work.

At the same time, he argued it was vital that 'policies aimed at disaffected boys are not introduced at the expense of girls whose improvement over recent years has been a real success story'. Despite such concerns about girls, many more recent projects have focused on how to raise boys' academic achievement, with noticeably less attention and funding being devoted to girls and Science/Mathematics after 16.

The Ofsted review's conclusion that 'there are no simple explanations for gender differences in performances; in any one context several factors are likely to have an influence' (Arnot *et al.* 1998) is reflected in the range of school approaches to gender equality developed in the UK. MacDonald *et al.*'s (1999) report on boys' achievement suggested that schools should take a whole-school approach to gender issues, putting into place a range of departmental strategies and management techniques, one of which is the annual monitoring of gender performance (SATS, GCSE and measures of value-added performance), or the targeting of particular pupils – particularly in Years 8 or 9. Short-term single-sex learning groups have been tried in mixed secondary schools in order to explore gender stereotypes about learning and to offer 'safe' contexts to review pupils' preferences and attitudes (e.g. in English). More opportunities have been provided in different subjects for boys and girls to explore their interests. Some schools have given more recognition to the need to work directly with boys and to build their confidence in themselves and their abilities. Teachers are now called upon to research for themselves how gender works within the culture and structure of the school, in relation, for example, to male and female responses to different teaching styles and learning demands, to different modes of assessment, and to various types of classroom organzation.

Blair *et al.* (1998), having investigated a number of successful multi-ethnic primary and secondary schools, found that what had made them effective was that they were 'listening schools'. These were schools that:

> ... took time to talk with students and parents; schools which were prepared to consider and debate values as well as strategies; schools which took seriously the views students and parents offered and their own interpretations of school processes; and schools which used this learning to reappraise, and where necessary change, their practices and to build a more inclusive curriculum. These schools did not assume the existence of ethnic stereotypes or indeed of fixed ethnic identities, but recognised the shared experiences of students in their evolving, culturally diverse communities. In this way, they were able to incorporate not only a respect for individuals but also for the collective or group identities to which students and their parents, in their own local context, had a sense of belonging. (p. 2)

The Ofsted (1999) report on school strategies in relation to ethnicity also picked up this theme, arguing that the most successful school approaches were associated with senior management making clear that the under-performance of any groups was not acceptable, that evidence was gathered systematically and that teachers and departments were challenged to 'spell out what they intend to do to improve the situation':

> The schools where minority ethnic pupils flourish understand the hostility these pupils often face ... These schools have developed successful strategies for countering stereotyping which have not only had a tangible impact on the pupils' confidence and self-esteem, but have also influenced the attitudes of the majority ...
>
> An important feature of successful race relations work is a school ethos which is open and vigilant, in which pupils can talk about their concerns and share in the development of strategies for their resolution. (Ofsted 1999, pp. 7–8)

As a result of the MacPherson Inquiry (1999) into the murder of Stephen Lawrence, schools are also being encouraged to ensure that they have clear policies for dealing with racial harassment. The Police Inspectorate have produced videos to help schools tackle racial incidents in schools, to help parents and carers of children who are experiencing racial harassment at schools, and to set up parent support groups.

Schools are aware of the controversies over, for example, the ways pupils are grouped (setting, streaming, banding and mixed ability teaching) and the need to encourage a learning culture in the school among all pupils. There are still many more debates to be had over the most appropriate organization of pupils, in order to ensure genuinely 'inclusive education' which allows each pupil to develop their abilities to the full. Other discussions are likely to focus on effective teaching approaches of successful black teachers (cf Callender 1997) in multiracial schools. Discussions about both 'inclusive education' and 'teaching for diversity' are especially relevant in a government climate which seeks to promote greater social cohesion as well as higher educational performances in schools. New ways of involving *all* pupils in learning are being sought therefore – not just in the new arenas of 'education action zones' but also by teachers keen to think creatively about the challenges schools are faced with today.

Improving the effectiveness of schools in relation to all their pupils is a task engaging teachers in a range of 'egalitarian' initiatives which involve thinking critically and constructively about gender, ethnic and social class patterns as part of the professional ethos and practice of teaching.

Chapter 9

Schools, Parents and the Community

TERENCE H. McLAUGHLIN

INTRODUCTION

Schools do not, and cannot, conduct their work in a vacuum, isolated from 'external' influences, forces and claims. It is not only practically impossible for schools to do this, but also wrong for them to try to do so. The 'external' factors with which schools are confronted involve not only influences and forces, but also *claims*. Some of these claims assert *rights* to (for example) information, consultation, shared decision-making or control. For reasons of principle as well as practical reasons a school must therefore attend to, and, where necessary, respond to 'external' realities and demands.

The 'external' realities and demands which surround the school are varied and wide-ranging, and they give rise to many complicated questions of a social, moral, political and economic kind. This chapter will focus attention upon two prominent sources of 'external' demand with respect to the school: parents and the community. Although there is much to be said about practical aspects of the relationship between schools, parents and the community, the emphasis here will be on some central matters of principle which arise.

It is useful to conduct our discussion in relation to a series of models of relationship between schools, parents and the community.

MODELS OF RELATIONSHIP BETWEEN SCHOOLS, PARENTS AND THE COMMUNITY

It is important to stress that the models presented here are 'ideal types' intended to act as a framework within which issues can be mapped. There is no suggestion that these models capture in any precise way the complex realities of existing relationships, either past or present.

1. Distance and separation

As its name implies, this model involves the school attempting to conduct its work, as far as possible, in a significantly isolated way from parents and the community. A model of this sort is discernible in relation to schools of all kinds in Britain, from the nineteenth century until relatively recently. Salient in this model is the notion of schools seeking to protect and even 'rescue' their students from the potentially negative influences of parents and communities. Victorian elementary schools often saw themselves as 'citadels of civilization' in the midst of wastelands of ignorance, poverty and squalor, a self-perception which was reflected in the architectural design of the school buildings. Grammar schools were often suspicious of the anti-educational influences of some parents and communities, and were particularly concerned to wean working-class students away from the potentially limiting and constraining effects of their home background. The elite public schools, particularly boarding schools, were keen to protect their students from possibly indulgent and decadent families who were seen as failing to instil in their children appropriate virtues of mind, character and leadership.

This model of 'distance and separation', particularly weaker forms of it, does not imply that schools were, or could be, completely isolated from parents and the community. The relationships involved were, however, often limited and restricted. Reports on pupil progress were often perfunctory, and parent involvement with the school was often restricted to invitations to be present at sports events, dramatic performances and the like.

It is possible to discern three broadly philosophical claims embedded in this model of relationship between schools, parents and the community:

1. That education is a kind of activity which is best conceived and pursued independently of the immediate surroundings, concerns and lives of the students. Education should be seen (in some sense) as 'academic'.
2. That educators (and, in particular, teachers) are in the best position to determine what is and what is not in the educational interests of students.
3. That it is appropriate to be suspicious of the educative influence of parents and the community.

All three of these claims are significantly controversial, and have been extensively challenged in recent years.

The view that education should be confined to 'academic' matters unrelated to the immediate surroundings, concerns and lives of students has been countered by the claim that education has an important part to play in the personal and social education of students, and that these aspects of education must necessarily make reference in various ways to the families of students and to the society in which they live. More generally, it has been argued that a fully rounded education requires ingredients which go beyond the merely academic. On motivational grounds alone, it has been claimed, education should relate to the existing interests, experience and interests of students and be (in some sense) 'relevant'. Education, therefore, cannot and should not be seen as 'distant' and 'separate' from life outside the school.

The view that educators (and, in particular, teachers) are in the best position to determine what is and what is not in the educational interests of students has been countered by the claim that whilst teachers have some professional expertise (particularly in relation to methods of teaching) this expertise does not encompass all that is required in order to determine the aims and 'content' of what is to be taught. The expertise required to determine these matters requires, among other things, the ability to answer such questions as: 'What knowledge is of most worth?' and 'In what ways should we shape the next generation?' These questions, like the question 'What kind of life is worth living?' are not ones which can be answered definitively by easily identified experts. In part this is because the questions are complex and in part because the questions involve judgements of value which are significantly controversial (for further discussion of matters of this kind see Chapter 11 in Part III of this volume). In a liberal democratic society, it has been argued, questions of this kind must be settled by wide-ranging discussion which includes parents and the community as a whole. Parents and the community therefore have rights to participate in educational decision-making, and teachers lack a mandate to settle all educational questions by themselves.

The view that it is appropriate to be suspicious of the educative influence of parents and the community has been countered by an acknowledgement of the potential educational benefits of this influence. In part this is seen in the beneficial effect on achievement which has been shown to follow from the well-conceived involvement of parents and the community in various aspects of teaching undertaken by the school. A prominent example of this kind of beneficial influence can be seen in the improvement in reading performance of pupils whose parents play a role in structured teaching programmes that have been developed in this area. The general point here is that parents and the community can offer to the school educational insights and resources of various kinds which it is unwise to ignore.

2. Mutual involvement

This model articulates the closer relationship between schools, parents and the community which is now common in contemporary educational practice and in educational legislation.

Five broadly philosophical claims can be discerned in this model:

1. That parents and the community be seen as having rights to appropriate forms of *information* about various aspects of the work of the school. The sorts of information involved here include details about the courses of study offered, the performance and progress of individuals, school policies and procedures of various kinds, school inspection reports and examination results.
2. That parents and the community be seen as having rights to engage in

consultation with the school on a range of matters of policy and principle such as (for example) the approach that the school should take to the handling of sensitive and significantly controversial issues such as sex education.

3. That parents and the community be invited to engage in *co-operation* with the school in relation to such matters as pupil learning (as in the example of parent assistance with reading improvement mentioned above), the educational programme offered by the school (as in a situation where local employers participate in various aspects of the school curriculum), and the provision of practical resources (as in fundraising of various kinds and the sharing of facilities such as swimming pools and playing fields between the school and the community).

4. That parents and the community be seen as having rights to engage in *shared decision-making* with the school on various matters of policy and practice through (for example) representation on governing bodies and on committees of local education authorities.

5. That schools be seen as having *a wider focus of educational concern* than the merely 'academic'. Thus, for example, personal and social education and the provision of appropriate forms of pastoral care are seen as part of the educative task of the school, and parents and the community are seen as important educational resources.

This model of the relationship between schools, parents and the community is supported by arguments of both a practical and a principled kind. On the practical side, it is clear that these forms of mutual involvement between schools, parents and the community are associated with greater educational effectiveness and efficiency. The beneficial effects of partnerships between schools and parents with respect to the promotion of aspects of student learning have already been mentioned. The financial and other efficiencies associated with facilities such as swimming pools jointly provided for schools and for communities are also noteworthy. However, the arguments supporting this model also have a principled character in that it is claimed that the model does justice to the *rights* which parents and the community have to the various forms of involvement which have been indicated.

Whilst each of the broadly philosophical claims associated with this model seem relatively unproblematic, questions and difficulties arise in relation to each of them. With regard to the claim about rights to the provision of information, for example, questions arise about the most appropriate way in which certain kinds of information should be provided. The publication of school 'league tables' based on examination results may give a misleading impression about the real educational performance of a school because the 'value added' element of the school's contribution (the extent to which the school has extended the achievements of its pupils since entry relative to their ability) may be invisible. Difficulties such as these generate a challenge to schools about how they can present information in a full and fair way to interested parties. Another specific issue which arises in relation to the provision of information concerns the possible controversiality of some information. Who, for example, should have access to the school records of individual pupils, and should all information held by the school be made available?

With regard to the claim about rights to engage in consultation, questions arise about how, where and on what grounds the line can be drawn between consultation and shared decision-making. The same questions arise in relation to the claim that parents and the community be invited to engage in co-operation with the school.

With regard to the claim about rights to shared decision-making, questions arise about which party should have the final say on matters which are disputed, and about the grounds on which the allocation of the final say should be determined in relation to the differing kinds of matter at stake.

With regard to the claim that schools should be seen as having a wider focus of educational concern than the 'academic', questions arise about the proper emphasis and priority to be given to various aspects of the educative task. These questions surface regularly in familiar and long-running educational disputes, some of which are expressed in terms of 'traditional' versus 'progressive' or 'academic' versus 'pastoral' conceptions of the educative role of schools.

3. Dominance of parents

This model embodies a conception of 'parents as determiner' with respect to their children's education. On this conception, parental rights in education are seen (within minimal limits) as fundamental, over-riding and extensive. There is a suspicion of the priority of 'professional' or 'political' judgement in educational matters and there may also be suspicion of a common form of educational provision offered by the state. The child's educational experience is seen as properly determined to the greatest possible extent by the child's own parents and family.

The model involves one major claim of a broadly philosophical kind:

• That parents have the capacity and right to exclusively determine what is in the educational interests of their children.

However, this claim has been subjected to a number of significant criticisms. A prominent line of criticism is that the most fundamental right which requires acknowledgement here is the child's 'right to an open future': a right of children to reach maturity '... with as many options, opportunities and advantages as possible' (Feinberg 1980, p. 130). This, it is argued, is the fundamental educational interest of the child which the parent has a duty to facilitate and which acts as an important limitation on parental rights. It involves (for example) parents avoiding the foreclosure of options for children through the making of certain 'crucial' or 'irrevocable' decisions determining the course of lives at too early a stage (*ibid.*, p. 143) and a requirement that children be provided with a broad education aimed at the development of their autonomy which acquaints them with '... a great variety of facts and diversified accounts and evaluations of the myriad human arrangements in the world and in history' (*ibid.*, p. 139). Another source of limitation on the 'parents as deter-miner' model of parents' educational rights is the rights and needs of other parents and of society. Among other things, this limitation generates the need to take account of imperatives of fairness and justice in the distribution of edu-cational goods, and the need to expand the educational entitlement of all pupils to include education for citizenship. (On education for citizenship see Chapter 13 by John Beck in Part III of this book.)

Arguments of this kind do not, of course, result in undermining all parental rights with respect to education. A more modest conception of the parent as 'trustee' of the child's educational rights can be readily defended. On this view, the parent has the right to determine the child's 'primary culture', including certain forms of separate schooling, and has the right to co-ordinate and review the educational experiences and development of the child. However, these educational rights are seen not as fundamental moral rights possessed by parents but rather as rights derived from parental duties to secure their children's autonomy and citizenship rights, which are merely 'held in trust' by parents until the child is capable of exercising them for him- or herself. Parents are not seen, therefore, as having fundamental moral rights which infringe the right of their children to achieve autonomy and formation as democratic citizens; nor do they have the right to infringe the rights and needs of other parents and of society. On this view, parents have important educational rights and are important agents in the various aspects of the 'mutual involvement' model which has been discussed. However, they are not seen as dominant in relationships between schools, parents and the community and they do not enjoy the role of an exclusive or wide-ranging 'determiner' with respect to their children's education (for further discussion of these matters see McLaughlin 1994a).

Acceptance of the general notion of 'parent as trustee' leaves room, however, for much detailed discussion about what precise parental rights can be derived from it.

4. Dominance of the educational marketplace

This model is often associated with the preceding one. Although it can take many forms, the essential feature of this model is the view that education is best provided through a 'marketplace' of different kinds of school, each com-peting for 'customers' (parents) who are in the possession of information and of resources (e.g. through possession of a 'voucher') to choose schools in line with their own educational desires. Included amongst the arguments in support of this model are those relating to the need to counteract compla-cency and inefficiency on the part of schools, and to provide an antidote to undue state power and monopoly in education.

Apart from the claim about the justifiability of the 'parents as determiner' conception of parental rights which has been discussed in the last section, this model involves at least one further broadly philosophical claim:

- That an educational market can best secure an adequate education for all.

Central to the evaluation of this claim is the question of how we should understand the notion of an 'adequate education'. Often, proponents of this model do not specify what is meant by 'adequate' here and suggest that this question should itself be determined by choices exercised within the marketplace. However, as we saw in relation to claims about parental rights, there are compelling reasons to think that there is an educational entitlement related to the development of personal autonomy and democratic citizenship which should be secured for all pupils. It is widely acknowledged that in the same way that the demands of the development of personal autonomy and democratic citizenship act as a brake upon parental rights, so they act as 'moral limits of the market'. The central issue between advocates and critics of markets in education then becomes: which system can best ensure the provision, not of some unspecified 'adequate' education whose definition is itself determined by the market, but the provision of this entitlement?

Given the relationship of this entitlement to fundamental matters of personal dignity and democratic agency, the duty of extending it to all children becomes clear. The question then takes on a more precise form: which system can best secure the provision of this entitlement for *all* children?

One difficulty which arises in relation to the claim that markets can secure this educational entitlement for all relates to doubts about whether all parents are in a position to seriously evaluate such an entitlement for purposes of choice. There is a danger that, in the situation of a significantly free educational market, parents will make unwise and limiting educational choices on behalf of their children. In the light of this, there seems to be a strong case for exempting this entitlement, if not other aspects of educational provision, from market forces, and securing its achievement for all pupils through forms of democratic state control and regulation (for further discussion of these matters see McLaughlin 1994b).

5. Dominance of the community

This model can take at least three forms, depending on how the notion of 'the community' is understood. The notion of 'the community' is capable of interpretation in a number of different senses. Three senses will be considered here, each related to variants of this model: the 'local' community, the 'culturally specific' community, and the 'general' community.

The 'Dominance of the Local Community' model is apparent (for example) in the vision of 'Village Colleges' developed by Henry Morris in Cambridgeshire in the 1930s (on this, see, for example, Ree 1973) and also in urban variants of this model developed in the 1960s and 1970s in comprehensive schools such as Sidney Stringer in Coventry, Stantonbury Campus in Milton Keynes and the Abraham Moss Centre in Manchester (on urban variants see, for example, Midwinter 1975). Common to all these models is a view of the need to link education closely with the local community, and to break down in a radical way the barriers between the local community and the school. One broadly philosophical claim which is associated with this model is as follows:

- That the local community should provide the focus for what is learnt in the school and be particularly salient in educational decision-making.

This claim is open to question on grounds of the potential narrowness and restrictiveness of what might result. In the light of the sort of educational entitlement for all which has been sketched earlier, why should attention be focused particularly upon local matters and why should educational decisions be made particularly at local level? The educational entitlement mentioned earlier seems to call in part for a national, international or even global perspective on certain matters; and the need for the entitlement to be secured for all seems to require consistency across potential variabilities between local differences. Relevant to these questions is the widely held view that a properly liberating education should lead pupils beyond 'the present and the particular' (on this notion see Bailey 1984). These arguments do not undermine the claim that local considerations should have a part to play in educational arrangements, as distinct from the more wide-ranging claim that these local considerations should be dominant.

'Culturally specific communities' include communities which exhibit (say) ethnic or religious distinctiveness, as in, for example, the Afro-Caribbean or the Muslim community within the UK. The 'Dominance of the Culturally Specific Community' model involves the following broadly philosophical claim, which is often expressed in relation to arguments for certain kinds of separate educational provision (for example, Muslim schools):

- That 'culturally specific communities' should have decisive educational decision-making rights in relation to the sort of educational experience which is appropriate for its children and young people.

This claim is open to question on a number of grounds. There are potential tensions between the claim and both the educational and other rights and needs of individuals who may be members of 'culturally specific communities', and the educational and other rights and needs of the broader community. A prominent line of argument is that whilst these 'culturally specific communities' can constitute 'primary cultures' in which children can be brought up, they should not completely prevent the sort of development of autonomy and democratic citizenship in individuals which has been alluded to, nor undermine the development of the sorts of general understandings and loyalties which society as a whole requires. Thus, it is claimed, whilst 'culturally specific communities' have an important role to play in educational decision-making (for example in illuminating what is required in a fair treatment of cultural diversity), it should not necessarily be a dominant role. The demands of the sort of educational entitlement which has been referred to, and which is closely related to the development of personal autonomy and democratic citizenship, must be borne in mind. Whilst these demands do not rule out the justifiability of certain sorts of separate school (on this matter see McLaughlin 1992), the demands do need to be taken into account in the overall judgements about educational policy and practice which need to be made.

The 'general' community can be regarded as the overall community in which individuals and citizens live. A 'liberal democratic' variant of 'The Dominance of the General Community' model involves the following broadly philosophical claim:

- That a liberal democratic society has the right and duty to ensure for all young people the sort of educational entitlement which is necessary for the achievement of personal autonomy and democratic citizenship.

Such a society may secure this entitlement through various strategies, including state control and regulation of education through (for example) a national curriculum. It is important to note that this variant of the model does not seek justification of state control over education of *any* kind. What is envisaged is control limited by the values and demands of the sort of educational entitlement which has been indicated, and subject to democratic discussion and mandate. There is no suggestion that the education envisaged on this model will be totalitarian or nationalistic in any objectionable sense. This may allay fears of state manipulation of, and indoctrination through, the educational system. Nor is the control envisaged seen as extending to all the details of the educational process, as distinct from its broad aims and framework. The model can accommodate, it is claimed, a proper role for teachers, parents, local communities and 'culturally specific' communities to contribute to educational decision-making. The role of the state, it is argued by supporters of this model, is simply to ensure that education satisfies its fundamental purposes.

An assessment of the adequacy of this model in principle needs to be separated from the particular features associated with the increased state control of education in England and Wales since 1988, which are not seen as necessarily corresponding to the principles which the model embodies. The philosophical claim which is made by the model is open to a number of lines of criticism. One of the most prominent of these is how the nature and limits of state control can be fleshed out in some detail, and how this control can be insulated from the potentially destabilizing effects of involvement in party political debates and processes (on this model see White 1990, Chs 1 and 9).

CONCLUSION

As indicated at the outset, the relationships between schools on the one hand and parents and the community on the other, give rise to many varied and complex questions of principle. Getting clearer about these matters of principle does not, and cannot, in itself settle all the equally varied and complex matters of practice which arise. Clarity may not be a sufficient requirement, but it is nevertheless a necessary requirement for an adequate approach to these important practical questions.

Given its centrality to much of our discussion, one of the central tasks in articulating a justifiable account of the principled relationship between schools, parents and the community is an articulation and defence of the notion of an educational entitlement related to the development of personal autonomy and democratic citizenship.

Chapter 10

Environmental Education: Education for Sustainable Development

MICHAEL YOUNGER AND ANGELA WEBSTER

ENVIRONMENTAL EDUCATION: EVOLUTION AND AIMS

Debates about the role and importance of environmental education within the secondary school curriculum have been around for a long time, and various attempts have been made to get environmental education more formally established on the curriculum. At different times, such attempts have been supported by pressure groups as diverse as the National Farmers' Union and Friends of the Earth, the Royal Institute of British Architects and the Women's Environmental Network. Environmental and rural studies, outdoor education, education for conservation and urban studies have each, in their own way, attempted to give a higher profile to environmental education, but progress has been slow, and there developed through the 1970s and 1980s curiously ambivalent relationships between the environmental education movement and established school subjects such as Geography, History and the sciences, which saw aspects of the environment as their own specialized, protected domain.

It is paradoxical in some respects that environmental education received more attention following the establishment of the National Curriculum in the years after the Education (No. 2) Act of 1986 and the Education Reform Act of 1988. It was almost as if policy-makers felt the need to balance a prescriptive, subject-oriented, content-laden curriculum with more open, cross-curricular perspectives. Whatever the rationale, the Curriculum Guidance booklets which emanated from the National Curriculum Council in 1990 identified environmental education as one of five cross-curricular themes, explicitly cross-referenced with the National Curriculum documents in History, Geography, Technology, the sciences, and also exploring the possibility of links with Drama, the arts and English. Such themes were intended to pervade the whole curriculum, encouraging schools to develop links between different aspects of their curriculum, and to develop a view of the curriculum as a whole. Many of the topics and themes with which they were concerned were central issues within the National Curriculum: the struggle for the tropical rainforests provided a cross-curricular theme for study in Geography, in Science, in Art, in Dance, in Drama, in English and in PSE; the water cycle, and issues of drought and pollution, were studied in Science and in Geography, in Technology and as a focus for Modern Language work; urban redevelopment and industrial regeneration featured in Maths, Technology, History, Geography and Religious Studies. Other aspects of environmental education focused upon skills and enquiry; thus town trails and streetwork exercises, for example, were designed to reveal the intrinsic interest and fine-grain of a relatively ordinary part of an urban environment, and to focus upon the potential of both unexceptional environments and 'typical' environments for environmental education. There was overt reference, too, to the gender angle, with studies of the urban built environment which focused on issues such as urban safety and mobility, and access to urban services.

The publication of Curriculum Guidance 7 (National Curriculum Council, 1990) raised the profile of environmental education nationally and brought the issue more centrally onto school curriculum planning agendas. Many schools responded by auditing their current practice, and there were expectations in some schools that each subject-based curriculum unit would include reference to cross-curricular themes. Other approaches involved cross-curricular events, such as environmental theatre projects and 'theme weeks', frequently with the support and involvement of organizations such as World Wildlife Fund for Nature, or the Body Shop. Although the NCC guidance was at no time translated into statutory prescription, there appeared nonetheless to be an emerging agreement on the scope and role of environmental education. Thus Duncan Graham, then the Chair of the NCC, could claim that: 'Environmental education is an essential part of every pupil's curriculum. It helps to encourage awareness of the environment, leading to informed concern for and active participation in resolving environmental problems.'

The same message of concern for raising student awareness, stimulating interest and understanding, and establishing a foundation for active participation in environmental issues, pervades Curriculum Guidance 7 itself:

> NCC recognises that environmental education is the subject of considerable debate and that there is no clear consensus about many of the issues. This makes it all the more important for pupils to have opportunities at school to learn the facts about the environment, to develop a respect for evidence, to clarify their own values in relation to the environment, and to understand that people hold different, equally legitimate points of view. Some of the issues are controversial, and it is important that they are presented to pupils in a balanced way, which recognises all points of view.

EDUCATION ABOUT, IN AND FOR THE ENVIRONMENT

As defined by the NCC, environmental education is perceived as having three closely integrated aspects. Education *about* the environment aims to develop a basic knowledge and understanding through the study of the environment, focusing on topics such as climate, soils and rocks, materials and resources, plants and animals, peoples and their communities. Such a perspective is concerned with the factual and conceptual understanding of environments at a variety of scales, seeking an understanding of the interactions which take place within environments, and examining the environment from a variety of viewpoints. As such, this perspective on environmental education puts the emphasis on increasing people's understanding of the multiplicity of factors which influence the environment, but at a level which acknowledges and accepts the existing social order and social relations. Growing out of a concern for environmental management, conservation and control, it adopts a mainly technocentric perspective to environmental education, presenting environmental issues as 'asocial or universal problems, which are rarely examined in terms of their structural causes' (Huckle 1990, p. 154).

Education *in and through* the environment stresses the use of the environment as a resource for learning experiences and the development of a broad range of enquiry, communication and participation skills. The environment is thus seen as a resource to give reality, relevance and practical experience to learning, with emphasis upon active enquiry and investigation in the field, developing skills and aesthetic responses. The emphasis is upon student-centred learning, fieldwork and enquiry which helps to develop an appreciation of the environment, 'education for environmental awareness and interpretation' (Huckle 1993a). This approach has a long-established pedigree in terms of giving a focus for discovery approaches to learning about the environment, and it has the potential to contribute to a raising of awareness and consciousness about the environment, without necessarily informing about the real causal processes which affect and govern the environment.

Education *for* the environment is envisaged as presenting pupils with opportunities to explore their personal response to environmental issues. Such an approach is concerned with considering ways of ensuring caring use of the environment now and in the future, considering solutions to environmental problems (taking into account that there are conflicting interests and differing cultural perspectives), and informing the choices which have to be made. This approach was initially developed on a small scale, focusing on local issues related to housing, environmental quality and congestion; some of the early work is described in issues of the *Bulletin of Environmental Education*, and in texts such as *Streetwork: The Exploding School* (Ward and Fyson 1973). Implicit within this work is a concern with values education, helping students to become active decision-makers and to develop a critical eye for environmental issues – all within a coherent and consistent framework of values. Taken to its logical conclusion, of course, this approach to environmental education inevitably focuses upon controversial issues, including issues about which there may be more societal conflict than consensus. At face value, the emphasis is not simply on heightening pupils' awareness of environmental issues and developing their aesthetic appreciation of environments, but on encouraging active participation in resolving environmental problems, of integrating all aspects to engender critical thinking, responsibility and action, in enabling students to 'think globally, act locally'. But Curriculum Guidance 7 itself was confused in emphasis; on the one hand stressing processes of learning and open-ended enquiry, it was nonetheless heavy on content. Not surprisingly, given the thrust of government policy at the time, it soon became clear that the official view of environmental education was that it should be more concerned with knowledge, understanding and skills than with active involvement and decision-making, or with reconciling rhetoric and practice.

SUSTAINABLE DEVELOPMENT AND EDUCATION

The concept of sustainable development came into the public domain following the UN Conference on the Human Environment in Stockholm in 1972. Global environmental crises began to make headline news throughout the Western world: the loss of tropical forests, the intensification of the nuclear debate following Chernobyl, atmospheric contamination on a vast scale in the form of increased acidity and greenhouse gas warming, growing alarm over the distribution of toxic chemicals in consumer goods – all emphasized clear messages of global environmental deterioration. Into the 1980s further concerns developed about population growth and the depletion of resources, and the incompatibility of economic growth with the preservation of environmental systems. The World Commission on Environment and Development (the Brundtland Commission), identified a series of overlapping crises which stemmed from a mismatch between the capacities of natural systems and human activities: a crisis of development, linked to poverty, nutrition and debt, particularly impacting upon countries of the South, and especially on women and children in those countries; a crisis of the environment, with insufficient resources to feed growing populations, a loss of biodiversity and forest resources, and resource degradation through misuse and pollution; a crisis of global insecurity, resulting in wars, conflict and refugee trails.

The notion of sustainability is thus defined as the capacity to meet the needs of the present without compromising the ability of future generations to meet their own needs. Within the concept, there is the recognition that economic growth is both desirable and possible, to meet the basic needs of humankind, but that it must be sustainable at a global level. Sustainable development emphasizes the need to reconcile economic development and conservation of the environment, and to place a consideration of environmental issues within a social, economic and political context. This concern with sustainability links with education *for* the environment, and gave a new impetus globally to environmental education. The Brundtland Report had itself emphasized the crucial role which the world's teachers had to play 'in helping to bring about the extensive social changes needed for sustainable development' (p. xiv), and Agenda 21, the programme for action following the UN Conference on Environment and Development (UNCED) in Rio in 1992, devoted similar attention to education for sustainability: 'Education is critical for promoting sustainable development, and improving the capacity of the people to address environmental and development issues' (UNCED 1992, Ch. 36, p. 2).

Such perspectives on environmental education for sustainability linked naturally with the rising concern for development education, with its integrative approach to global issues and its commitment to experiential styles of learning, and also to developing the culture of co-operation in the classroom (see, for example, the seminal work of the Centre for Global Education (Pike and Selby 1988).) Focusing initially on 'Third World' poverty, development education evolved in such a way as to enable development and under-development to be explored as one and the same process, impacted upon by global economic and political systems. As inequalities between North and South, and within and between countries of the South, became increasingly evident, so the development education focus on distributive justice, and meeting the basic human needs of all the population, became more emphatic. Linked to this were the notions of equity and social justice, highlighting the distribution of a country's income and services among its peoples, and stressing equality of access for all regardless of age, status, gender or ethnicity. The focus upon development education also emphasized, if further emphasis were needed, the link between poverty and environmental issues, and the need to consider such issues within economic and cultural perspectives.

In this overall context, then, sustainable education can be seen as a process which, as well as stressing the inter-dependence of peoples and environments through the globe, 'develops people's awareness . . . , attitudes and values, enabling them to be effectively involved in sustainable development at local, national and international level, and helping them to work towards a more equitable and sustainable future' (Sterling *et al.* 1992).

ENVIRONMENTAL EDUCATION FOR SUSTAINABILITY

Such approaches to environmental education for sustainability embody a number of challenges to teachers and to teacher educators. At a basic level, while there can be no doubt that there has been a seismic shift in public attitudes to the environment in the past decade, there is still an enormous ignorance about environmental issues. Studies of trainee teachers' knowledge of the greenhouse effect, the ozone layer and acid rain revealed significant gaps in understanding, and showed that student awareness and knowledge of environmental concepts was frequently superficial and lacked an understanding of causal chains (Dove 1996). Many experienced teachers, responding to such issues mainly from a subject-specific perspective, feel under-prepared to tackle issues which are so complex, multi-faceted and subjective.

It is in defining the essential nature of environmental education for sustainability (EEFS), however, that we expose the full extent of the challenge to teachers. EEFS is not only concerned with generating an understanding of the concept of global interdependence, of a global ecosystem in which the future of all species, humans included, is inextricably interlinked, but with embracing a commitment to action based on such understanding – a commitment to change. There *is* a concern within society, a belief held by many and particularly by children, that the preservation of environmental quality is important, but few extend this to a consideration of how their own consumption patterns and ways of living might need to change if environmental sustainability is to be achieved. The challenge for EEFS is to translate a generalized concern for the environment into an understanding that it involves personal costs and constraints, and this means developing both understanding *and* commitment. This point is well developed by Tilbury:

> In order to contribute to EEFS, environmental work will need to be relevant to the student, through increasing their understanding of themselves and the world around them. It must encourage pupils to explore links between their personal lives and wider environmental and development concerns, by dealing with issues such as consumerism, and how the practices of banking and industry affect their lives. (Tilbury 1995, p. 199)

Similarly, Fien, in outlining an environmental and development education project for teacher educators in Australia, identifies the fundamental questions which have to be faced:

> Issues of environment, social justice and sustainable development pose important questions for the future of human society ... those involved in environmental and development education, at whatever level, need to activate the socially critical or reconstructionist tradition in education and promote approaches to curriculum planning and pedagogy that can help integrate social justice and ecological sustainability into a vision and a mission of personal and social change. (Fien 1995, p. 25)

In this context, it is clear that EEFS raises a number of uncomfortable challenges for schools and politicians. Young teachers have a number of explicit issues to consider when learning to teach about environmental issues: they 'have to select appropriate subject matter and teaching strategies, decide on their aims for students' values education and decide on their own role as teachers in handling controversial issues with their students' (Corney 1998, p. 90). It is Corney's emphasis on teaching strategies and controversial issues that is of central concern here. EEFS gives legitimacy to concerns with affective, value-based responses, as well as with cognitive understanding; such teaching acknowledges that children are to be given opportunities to develop their own value-based responses, and recognizes that we are concerned with teaching about issues which may engender conflict and controversy. Handled skilfully by experienced teachers, this might not be too problematic, but at another level, such a focus for environmental education, with the central concern on values and attitudes, is complex and challenging, and many teachers feel ill-equipped, in terms of their own teaching strategies, to cope with such issues. Even for experienced teachers, a major concern is the lack of extensive teacher support materials with activities to boost confidence in handling controversial issues in the classroom.

But there is a still further issue of concern. Central to the concept of sustainability is a holistic approach to the study of the environment and development issues, an approach which stresses global inter-dependence, and interactions between people and their whole environment : 'Many definitions of environmental education lay emphasis on interconnectedness, interdisciplinarity and viewing the environment in its entirety ... consistent with a holistic perspective' (Sterling 1993, p. 74). In many countries, however, the approach to teaching about environmental issues is fragmentary, unco-ordinated, and usually discipline-based (Huckle 1993b). Ironically, in the United Kingdom context, such moves as there were towards an integrated approach to environmental education were hindered and in some instances overthrown by the implementation of the subject-specific National Curriculum after 1988. Similarly, the content-heavy nature of such curricula meant that there was less time and space for innovative teaching strategies which had the capacity to be adapted for EEFS teaching. Thus work associated with the Humanities Curriculum Project, and teaching methodologies central to the ethos of Schools Council projects such as Geography for the Young School-Leaver and the Schools' Council History Project, with their emphasis on discussion, open-ended enquiry, simulations and values exploration, became less pivotal and influential, at the very time when they had the capacity to transform environmental education teaching. Where environmental education was given recognition, the emphasis was too often upon didactic teaching methods and fact-gathering, receptive learning approaches (Gayford 1991), upon transmission modes of teaching which gave low priority to open and controversial areas of knowledge, and downgraded crucial issues which crossed disciplinary boundaries and could not be contained within a specific subject .

Hence in the United Kingdom there is the fundamental paradox: on the one hand, successive governments have subscribed to and advocated environmental sustainability at the international and national policy level, and promoted EEFS as an important component of this strategy; at the same time, a prescriptive, subject-based, content-oriented National Curriculum has been imposed upon schools which has severely limited the scope and the methodologies available for teaching EEFS. Despite the publication of Curriculum Guidance 7, environmental education lost ground in the United Kingdom's schools in the last decade. As the education system shifted its focus to an emphasis on raising standards defined in terms of knowledge and understanding, aspects of affective education, including beliefs, values and attitudes, received less attention and prominence.

The extent of the challenge is clear: how have teachers and teacher educators responded to it? From the time of the Humanities Curriculum Project and its advocacy of the teacher as a neutral chair, environmental education has faced the challenge of devising strategies through which to teach about controversial environmental issues, whilst avoiding the promotion of the teacher's own values and opinions. Approaches have been sought which have allowed students to understand certain controversies, whilst appreciating the range of perspectives available, and gaining an expectation that there is not necessarily one right answer.

The emphasis upon values education is one such approach, for it is clear that central to environmental education is the difficult and politically sensitive task of helping children to develop a more sophisticated and critical understanding of the values that inform everyday life (Bonnett 1997). Here the emphasis on enquiry as a route to personal beliefs and actions (Naish *et al.* 1987) gives students opportunities to use discussion and logical analysis of evidence, to analyse and investigate real issues with a values dimension (e.g. values analysis as defined by Fien and Slater 1985). It enables students to focus on opinion, to explore the possibility of prejudice and bias, and to consider stages in decision-making about environmental issues. But it also allows students opportunities to come to a personal decision and judgement, to help them become aware of their own values in relation to their behaviour and that of others (values clarification), and offers the possibility of a personal response. In this context, it is analogous to active learning,

> encouraging students to see themselves as interacting members of social and environmental systems, through having them clarify and analyse values with the intention of enabling them to act in relation to social and environmental issues according to their value choices. (Fien and Slater 1985)

Other approaches have involved the production of workshop materials for teachers and teacher educators, which have aimed to develop critically reflective teachers who have a sound grasp of the debates linked to sustainability, and who are enabled to involve pupils in action-research learning through teaching strategies such as simulations, role plays, games and discussion. In Australia, this approach has been adopted by the environmental and development education project for teacher educators entitled *Teaching for a Sustainable World* (Fien 1995), and in the United Kingdom the Worldwide Fund for Nature spearheaded an in-service education initiative, *Reaching Out: Education for Sustainability* (Huckle *et al.* 1995), which provided a comprehensive course in the theory and practice of EEFS. Handled well, such strategies can give students some insights into the culture-laden aspects of many environmental issues, allowing for discussion of these issues within economic contexts, and giving scope for appreciating the different values of other, non-European, non-white cultures. The emphasis on 'futures education' (Hicks 1994; Hicks and Holden 1995) is a further aspect which needs consideration. At one level, the study of environmental issues and problems can lead to feelings of despair and helplessness, to indignation and compassion fatigue, whereas 'encouraging students to explore their preferred futures can lead to greater feelings of hope and empowerment' (Hicks and Holden 1995).

CONCLUSION

There has been little opportunity here to consider the aesthetics of environments, but implicit within EEFS is the assumption that the world is worth sustaining! As our home, and essential to our survival, the point needs little development. But a consistently neglected aspect of environmental education has been the concern with the quality of *individual* places and localities, a consideration not only of the cognitive but of the aesthetic and the spiritual. Thus each of us has our own sense of place, a subjective, unique interpretation of place, which frequently defies rationality and logic. Images from literature, music and art, feelings and emotions linked to sights, sounds and smells of a place; intangibles linked with experiences and half-forgotten memories, all contribute to our subjective impression of place, to a perception of place which is both real and unreal, and which is an essential part of our being. Each of us has that special place, which quickens the heartbeat, which excites: a place which perhaps we retreat to, in mind if not always in body, which revives and sustains us. No environment now exists in isolation from humankind; environments have different meanings for different people, in time and space. We respond to environments differently, we evaluate them differently. Given this, we need to be aware that one of the tasks of environmental education is to open up environments and places for students, to encourage them to explore their own feelings, emotions and understandings of environments and places, to allow them experiences, encounters and opportunities whereby they will develop a sense of place and an understanding of valued environments.

The last decade has seen an increasing national and international prominence given to issues of sustainability. Educational policies within the United Kingdom have been at odds with these environmental policies, however, and despite the efforts of a number of radical educationalists, teaching for environmental education still focuses heavily upon didactic and knowledge-oriented approaches. There remains the challenge of developing effective and flexible teaching resources and strategies which allow students to consider value- and issue-based environmental challenges in a critical way. Such approaches will have the potential to reduce the sense of powerlessness and frustration which are often generated by a study of environmental problems, and sustain a continuing interest and involvement in environmental issues.

It needs to be explicitly acknowledged, however, that the aims of environmental education for sustainability go beyond an exploration of students' value positions and their understanding of current debates about sustainability. Earlier work on values education, particularly in the context of geography and the humanities, placed the emphasis on the valuing process and on 'values probing', on students clarifying their own value positions and acting consistently within their own values framework. Such an approach enabled students to consider the implications of the environment and society of alternative courses of action, to make judgements about the respective merits of such actions, and to decide their own responses, behaviour and future courses of action in relation to sustainable living. (Corney and Middleton 1996, p. 329)

But the aims of EEFS go further than this, than simply providing students with a process whereby they come to an independent value position:

EEFS does not merely hope that learning activities will lead to the development of an (environmental) ethic. Instead it sets out positively to develop environmental awareness and concern to a level which will result in the acquisition of a personal environmental ethic ... teachers actively promote the consideration of values required for the development of sustainable lifestyles and do not hold a neutral stance. (Tilbury 1995, pp. 201–2)

From such a perspective, the analogy with education about issues of race, gender and disability is very clear.

Part III

**Values, Citizenship,
Personal, Social and Health Education**

Chapter 11

Values in Education

TERENCE H. McLAUGHLIN

INTRODUCTION

Education cannot be value-free. Every action (and every omission) of a teacher is value-laden and so is every aspect of the ethos and organization of the school. Education is inherently saturated with value. Since education cannot be value-free, we cannot therefore avoid fundamental questions such as: *which* values should education embody and transmit, *why?* and *how?*

What is meant by the term 'value'? Although much more needs to be said about this question, for the purposes of the present chapter values can be regarded in a rather broad way as criteria (standards or principles) for judging worth. There are, of course, many things which may be valued or judged worthy (including, for example, personal qualities, forms of understanding and states of affairs) and many respects and aspects in which they may be seen to be valuable or of worth. A significant range of values are of relevance and importance for education.

EDUCATION AND THE INESCAPABILITY OF VALUES

The inescapability of values in education is obvious. Let us reflect on the activity of the teacher in the classroom. In seeking to bring about learning, the teacher engages in a wide range of activities including describing, explaining, initiating discussion, prescribing study-related tasks, encouraging, admonishing and the like. All these complex and inter-related activities presuppose that the kind of learning which is being aimed at is thought valuable in some way. The teacher of History, for example, assumes that it is valuable for students to study history in general and valuable that the students study the specific periods and aspects of history which are being taught. Further, the teacher assumes the value of the particular kinds of learning within history which he or she wishes to promote (the achievement of an empathetic understanding of forces and motives, say, as well as a knowledge of facts). In addition, since teachers do not only teach their own subject, but impart wider lessons about (say) learning in general and about matters relevant to the individual, social and moral development of students, the value of what is taught in these wider lessons is also assumed. As well as presupposing the value of *what* is taught, teaching also involves value presuppositions about *how* teaching should be conducted. Not all ways of bringing about learning are educationally desirable or acceptable, and educational values must be appealed to in determining what educational desirability or acceptability amounts to here. It is necessary to acknowledge that in teaching it is not easy to separate 'what' is being taught from 'how' it is being taught; in many cases 'how' lessons are taught constitute 'lessons' in themselves. These remarks about the value-laden nature of teaching apply also to the life and work of the school. Its aims and processes are value-laden in similar ways.

It is important to note that attempts sometimes made by teachers and schools to be 'neutral' or 'non-judgemental' with respect to matters of value, involve not the absence of value judgements but the presence of complex ones. For example, teachers may feel for various reasons that they should not express their own views to students on certain controversial issues, or judge that they lack a mandate to teach or transmit a specific value stance to students on such matters. However, the forbearance of expression and influence on the part of teachers in cases like these is far from being value-free. A teacher who is reluctant to tell students whether God exists or whether a given political party has the correct approach to a particular matter is not seeking to abdicate all value responsibility. On the contrary, such a teacher is trying to transmit to students certain 'value messages'. These 'value messages' include the need for students to think and judge for themselves about significantly controversial matters, and for students to recognize the limits of the expertise and mandate of the teacher in relation to such questions.

The value-laden character of the activities of teaching and schooling (and more broadly of education) is not merely a matter of practical inescapability: it is also one of logic. A value-free education is not merely a practical impossibility but also a contradiction in terms. The very idea of education involves value.

THE PERVASIVENESS OF EDUCATIONAL VALUES

Values in education are pervasive. Education in values is taking place in everything that a teacher says and does (and in everything that a teacher does not say and do) and in all the aspects of the life and work of the school. It is far from the case, therefore, that education in values takes place only when 'value issues' are explicitly addressed with students, as in specifically designed and labelled lessons or course units, for example. Nor are 'value issues' uniquely and exclusively associated only with certain subjects and topics.

It is vital to realize that the value influence on students exerted by teachers and schools is not confined to influence which is deliberately intended. Unintended value influence can take place through the 'hidden curriculum' of teaching and schooling, and in some cases this influence can contradict and undermine what teachers and schools intend. Thus, for example, various forms of unacknowledged prejudice may infect a teacher's interactions with some pupils, and cast doubt on claims that all members of the student body are being treated with equal respect. Further, rigid policies of setting and streaming on the part of the school may give the lie to the claim that equality of opportunity is being provided for all. It is therefore necessary for the value influence exerted by teachers and schools to be kept under careful and sensitive review.

THE VARIETY AND COMPLEXITY OF EDUCATIONAL VALUES

We often tend to assume, in speaking of educational values, that we are referring to moral values. Educational values, however, are of many different kinds. Moral values and moral education are only a part, albeit an important part, of the 'value responsibility' of teachers and schools. (For a fuller discussion of moral values in education see Chapter 12.)

The values inherent in the aims, content, processes and achievements of education are wide ranging. They include judgements about human good implicit in general educational ideals and aims (for example, the ideal of personal autonomy or of the 'active citizen'), particular judgements within subjects or areas of study (such as the criteria for a good poem or an adequate scientific explanation) and commitments of a social and political kind (seen, for example, in policies aimed at equality of opportunity in its various aspects). Even if these broader educational values have moral aspects or implications, they extend beyond the moral to include values which are intellectual, aesthetic, social and political in nature.

There are a number of complexities which arise in relation to educational values. Five complexities are worthy of mention here. First, the fact that educational values are so pervasive and varied makes it difficult for us to discuss them with any degree of clarity and coherence. A persistent temptation when discussing educational values is to fall into 'edu-babble' (a form of imprecise and platitudinous rhetoric similar to psycho-babble). Yet it is important for teachers and schools to bring questions relating to educational values clearly into focus, not simply at the level of theory and principle but also at the level of practical implications for the classroom and school. A second complexity relates to the fact that not all educational values are mutually consistent or harmoniously realizable. They can conflict with each other and therefore call for judgements about priority and emphasis. Examples of such conflicts include the tensions between freedom and equality in education and between breadth and depth of study. A third complexity relates to the diversity and dispute which arises in relation to at least some educational values. This matter will be considered in more detail below. A fourth complexity concerns the question: who should properly determine educational values – teachers, schools, students, parents, the state, the local community, the democratic community as a whole, employers, or the mechanisms of an educational marketplace? Teachers and schools do not, and cannot, conduct their work in a vacuum, isolated from other influences, forces and claims. Fifth, and as a consequence of the preceding four complexities, it can be very difficult for teachers and schools to develop an approach to educational values which is unified and coherent.

VALUES, EDUCATION AND CONTROVERSIALITY

Teachers and schools exercise influence not only upon the thoughts and minds of students, but also on their wider development as persons. In an important sense, education shapes persons and their lives. It is therefore appropriate and necessary for the values inherent in education to be carefully assessed by teachers, parents and the community more generally. Many values with which education is concerned are relatively uncontroversial in that they enjoy widespread support from informed academic and professional opinion and from parents and the community as a whole. It is important not to over-emphasize controversiality in relation to educational values. A reasonable and well-grounded consensus exists on many issues. In the area of morality, for example, few doubt that teachers should urge their students to respect other people and their property, to be honest and responsible, to exercise self-control and to be fair and just. The immorality of bullying and child abuse, for example, is not in doubt. A reasonable and stable consensus also exists in relation to many other educational values. The general nature of a balanced curriculum and of appropriate teaching processes, for example, are the subject of wide agreement.

However, education is an area which does give rise to significant controversy. The notion of *significant* controversy is worthy of emphasis here. Not all disagreements and disputes are significantly controversial. Some disagreements and disputes arise from misunderstanding and ill-will. Significant controversy exists when contrasting views on an issue are based on well-grounded and non-trivial differences of judgement, and where these contrasting views are not contrary to reason. Significant controversy may exist for various reasons. Sufficient evidence to settle the matter at stake may not yet be available; the weighting or interpretation to be given to evidence or aspects of evidence may not be agreed; what counts as evidence may be in dispute and (in the most wide-ranging cases of disagreement) whole contrasting frameworks of understanding, belief and value may be at stake. A complexity here is that what actually constitutes a matter of significant controversy can itself be a matter of significant controversy.

Some matters of educational controversy do not appear to involve matters of value directly but seem to take the form: if we value the learning of X by students, what is the best way to bring that learning about? Caution is needed, however, in relation to educational disputes which appear to be merely 'technical' – about means rather than ends. We noted earlier that it is not easy to separate 'what' is being taught from 'how' it is taught. 'Means' and 'ends' are often inseparable in an educational context. A dispute about the best way to teach a given subject matter may be partly evaluative in character. Disputes between 'traditionalists' and 'progressives' in education, for example, often involve competing evaluations of what is to count as learning of the appropriate kind.

Other educational disputes have a more directly evaluative character, as in the famous question of Herbert Spencer: 'Which knowledge is of most worth?' Disputes of this more directly evaluative kind are found at different levels. Spencer's question is at the most general level, where disputes about different conceptions (or 'philosophies') of education are to be found. Familiar disputes here concern the aims and 'content' of education (for example, about the relative importance of traditional academic disciplines, study 'relevant' to 'life' and to social and personal development, vocational preparation, and breadth versus depth in study); the processes of education (for example, about how the role of the teacher in its different aspects should be conceived); and about matters of institutionalization and control (for example, about the extent to which diversity of schooling should be permitted or encouraged and about the extent of the rights of choice of parents). Often, particular evaluative assumptions are built into the language we are invited to use in relation to education (terms such as 'delivery', 'input/output' and 'learning outcomes' are clearly value-laden in this way). Evaluative disputes do not merely arise at the most general level of educational thinking, policy-making and practice; they are manifest in different ways at all levels.

Adequate attention to the full range of questions which arise in relation to educational values requires extensive discussion. Henceforth, this chapter will focus attention upon one specific question: the principles which should govern the teaching of controversial value issues in schools.

EDUCATION AND THE TEACHING OF CONTROVERSIAL VALUE ISSUES

In the light of our earlier discussion it is clear that the explicit handling of controversial value issues is only one aspect of the overall 'value influence' of schools. It is also clear that not all value issues explicitly dealt with in the curriculum give rise to significant controversy. Any education worthy of the name, however, cannot ignore significant value disagreement in its different aspects. It has recently been insisted, for example, that an examination of controversial issues is an inescapable part of Education for Citizenship (Qualifications and Curriculum Authority 1998, Section 10). (For further discussion of Education for Citizenship see Chapter 13.) The need for the explicit handling of significantly controversial issues does, however, arise in relation to a number of aspects of the curriculum of the school. Whilst personal, moral, social, political and religious issues notably give rise to well-grounded and non-trivial disagreement, such disagreement is not confined to these matters. In the approach of teachers and schools to significant value disagreement the following general considerations are relevant.

Liberal democracy, diversity, and public/non-public values

We are confronted in modern liberal democratic societies by people holding many different, and often incompatible, values, including 'comprehensive' theories of the good, or overall views of life. Catholics, Jews and Muslims live alongside atheists and agnostics. These comprehensive views are significantly controversial because, it is claimed, there is no way of objectively and conclusively adjudicating between them to the satisfaction of all citizens. Nor are these disagreements likely to be conclusively resolved in the future. They are deep seated and tenacious, the result of fundamental differences of belief and value. Yet many of these comprehensive theories of the good can be regarded as 'reasonable' or 'within the moral pale'. They do not conflict with, even if they go beyond, values acceptable to all. Liberal democratic societies, and the philosophical theory of liberalism in terms of which they are frequently articulated, approach questions of value diversity by invoking a distinction between 'public' and 'non-public' values and spheres.

The nature of this distinction is illuminated by the observation by Jonathan Sacks in his 1990 Reith Lectures, that in modern democratic societies, people 'speak' two 'languages of evaluation': a 'first' language of public (or common) values and a 'second' language of their own substantial traditions reflected in familial, religious and cultural communities (Sacks 1991).

'Public' values can be regarded as those which, in virtue of their fundamentality or inescapability, are seen as binding on all persons. Frequently embodied in law and expressed in terms of rights, they include such matters as basic social morality and a range of democratic principles such as freedom of speech and justice. 'Public' values can be affirmed by persons whose wider frameworks of beliefs differ from each other. They do not presuppose some particular metaphysical theory of the self, or of the nature of human destiny. For example, atheists and Catholics differ profoundly on such matters, but they can share common ground in condemning cruelty and supporting a democratic way of life, even if their different overall frameworks of belief give them a distinctive perspective on such matters. It is the 'public' values which constitute the common or unifying values which are necessary for a democratic society and on which its characteristic notions of pluralism and multiculturalism depend. 'Public' values, in virtue of their fundmentality and inescapability, give wide-ranging relativism pause for thought.

In contrast to the 'public' values, 'non-public' values go beyond what can be affirmed by, and insisted upon for, all members of a society. They are part of a range of options from which, within a framework of justice, persons might construct their lives. Such values may involve wide-ranging views of life as a whole, such as a religious faith or a substantial political creed. Since such 'comprehensive' theories of the good are significantly controversial, they cannot be imposed or insisted upon for all members of society but are seen as matters for individual and family assessment and decision. It is in relation to these 'non-public' values that the notion of 'respected difference' associated with pluralism and multiculturalism arises, and the difficulties with evaluation to which relativism presents itself as a response.

The distinction between 'public' and 'non-public' values, and the precise determination of the 'content' of each of the categories, is not without difficulty. The distinction is, however, helpful in discerning principles for the handling of significantly controversial matters in schools (for further discussion see McLaughlin 1995a).

Pluralism and multiculturalism

Two other concepts which are often encountered in relation to the discussion of significantly controversial value issues are pluralism and multiculturalism. Both notions, however, need to be carefully understood. They point not only to the mere existence of diversities of various kinds within a liberal democratic society but also to the need for these diversities to be (in some sense) positively valued.

In discussions of pluralism and multiculturalism, emphasis is often laid on the significance of diversity. It is important to note, however, that the very notions of pluralism and multiculturalism imply elements of commonality as well as diversity. Without common values, ideals and procedures, a pluralist multicultural society would not only disintegrate but would also lack, among other things, freedom, equality and tolerance: values essential to pluralism and multiculturalism themselves, as well as to democracy. The respects in which pluralism and multiculturalism involve a balance of unifying and diversifying elements is well brought out in the vision of a democratic, pluralist, multicultural society outlined in the report of the Swann Committee of Enquiry into the Education of Children from Ethnic Minority Groups (Great Britain, House of Commons 1985, Ch. 1).

One of the central questions raised by the notions of pluralism and multiculturalism is the nature and extent of the diversity which should be valued, and on what grounds. Clearly, there is nothing about diversity or difference *per se* which is valuable. Murder, theft and exploitation are aspects of diversity. Clearly only *certain sorts* of diversity are candidates for favourable evaluation. What, however, does 'favourable evaluation' mean here? Is the diversity at issue to be judged worthy merely of toleration, or of some more full-blooded acceptance?

Relativism

A general attitude or perspective which is often encountered in relation to the discussion of significantly controversial value issues is relativism. Relativism is the view that judgements of value (and, possibly, also of knowledge and truth) are relative to, and dependent upon, such variables as time, place, society, culture, moral code, practices, forms of life, conceptual schemes or frameworks, and personal background, circumstances and perspective. In its most extreme forms, relativism holds that there are no general standards or criteria of evaluation and no neutral or objective ways of choosing between the different sets of standards or criteria associated with these relative variables. There are no objective values, but merely *my* or *your* or *their* values. Among the educational consequences of relativism is an undermining of the point of discussing alternative views with the aim of rationally evaluating these views and not merely becoming aware that they exist.

However, the extreme claim that all values are relative, and that it is impossible to appeal to any well-grounded basis on which we can claim that some values are better or more adequate than others, is both overstated and incoherent. The claim is overstated because it overlooks the extent of the reasonable consensus on many value questions which was alluded to earlier. It is incoherent, because in calling into question in a radical way the value of, say, general standards of argument, the claim does not provide any grounds on which it can itself make sense. The claim presents itself as stating something which is true (that there are no valid general standards of argument). But if there are no standards of truth or argument, how can the claim be coherently articulated, given that it involves an argument about what is true? A perspective of thoroughgoing relativism, apart from its inherent difficulties, makes the task of education both impossible and incoherent.

A rejection of an extreme form of relativism leaves us, however, with the question of how precisely we should approach matters of evaluation in relation to significantly controversial issues.

Differing schooling contexts and mandates for value influence

The general mandate for the exercise of value influence which is enjoyed by schools of all kinds can be roughly expressed in the following way. All schools, regardless of their character, are on firm ground in presupposing and transmitting the 'public' values which have been referred to. Schools do not regard the morality of bullying or racism as open questions and nor do they hesitate to promote democratic values such as respect and toleration (within principled limits) for the views and decisions of others. Day by day, schools of all kinds urge their students to respect other people and their property, to be honest and responsible, to exercise self-control, to think for themselves and to achieve appropriate forms of autonomy in relation to many matters. 'Public' values such as these can be regarded as fundamental or basic: they are constitutive of civilized life in any human community – and, more specifically, in a democratic one – and are therefore in a sense 'non-negotiable' for any school. These values are 'shared', not in the sense that every person shares them – murderers and despots do not – but that they are not matters for reasonable and civilized dispute.

What value influence should schools exert with respect to the more complex and controversial value issues which are characteristic of the 'non-public' domain? What, for example, should schools say about the truth or otherwise of a particular religion, the adequacy of a particular code of sexual ethics or the coherence of the policy of a political party on a matter of contemporary interest? Here it is important to note the differing mandates for value influence enjoyed by different kinds of school. 'Common' schools are intended for students of all backgrounds and are not based on a particular 'view of life'. Since the value influence exerted by such schools must be broadly acceptable to society as a whole, they lack a mandate to present values in the significantly controversial 'non-public' domain as if they were unequivocally true and good. Rather the mandate of the common school is seen as that of illuminating the nature of the controversies which arise and of helping students to explore, understand, discuss and make critically reflective judgements of their own about the matters at stake. In contrast, 'separate' schools, which are based on a particular 'view of life' (usually a religious one) enjoy a mandate to exercise more wide-ranging value influence in the 'non-public' domain than their 'common' counterparts. Thus Anglican and Catholic schools, for example, enjoy a mandate to form their students in a particular religious faith, together with the ethical, social and political sensibility associated with it. Such schools, do not, of course, enjoy a mandate to crudely indoctrinate, and they face the challenge of offering their distinctive value influence to students in a way which respects the demands of criticism and personal autonomy (for more discussion of common and separate schools respectively see McLaughlin 1995b and 1992).

TEACHING APPROACHES AND STRATEGIES IN RELATION TO CONTROVERSIAL VALUE ISSUES

A number of approaches and strategies can be discerned in relation to the teaching of significantly controversial value issues. These include ignoring or evading the issues, seeking balance, adoption of a form of procedural neutrality, invoking the notions of reasonableness and impartiality, and engaging in counter-advocacy. These approaches and strategies all require assessment in the light of the principles and considerations discussed in the last section. (For a detailed discussion of particular approaches and strategies and related ideas see, for example, Bridges 1986, Qualifications and Curriculum Authority 1998, Section 10.)

CONCLUSION

This chapter has confined itself to a discussion of some of the key issues which arise in relation to values in education from a philosophical perspective. Philosophy alone, however, cannot deal with all the issues which arise in relation to educational values, much less determine the practical implications for teachers, schools and educational policy-makers which arise. Educational values require illumination from many academic perspectives (including sociological, psychological and historical ones) and from the practical insights and experience of those working in classrooms and schools. Philosophical considerations of the sort which have been outlined, however, have an indispensible role to play in our understanding of educational values and the practical implications and demands to which they give rise.

Chapter 12

Moral Education

CHRISTINE TUBB

INTRODUCTION

Few would deny that schools have a part to play in moral education, but exactly what that means is elusive. Many people have an expectation that 'teachers should be contributing more directly to the promotion of moral values appropriate to the creation and maintenance of an orderly and law-abiding society' (Best and Lang 1997, p. vii). Perhaps, in the wake of intense media attention focused on recent crimes of violence committed by children, they feel that a significant number of young people somehow lack all sense of morality and that schools ought to simply teach children what is right and wrong.

QUESTIONABLE UNDERLYING ASSUMPTIONS

In examining whether or not schools should attempt to satisfy this demand, it is important to be aware of some underlying assumptions and the questions they raise. There appears to be, for example, an implicit conviction that there is a direct causal relationship between knowing what is right and refraining from crime. However, it is not obvious that people generally act in morally objectionable ways because they do not know what they ought to do. Even murderers rarely seem to be confused about the morality of murder. They do not argue that murder is good, but in defence are more likely to claim that they were not responsible, that there was no choice on this particular occasion, or that a particular incident was not a case of murder, but an accidental killing or manslaughter.

Sometimes people can have clear conceptions of right and wrong and yet be weak – failing to live up to their moral principles; at other times they may be intentionally doing wrong as a protest or a means of rebellion. None of this is incompatible with *knowing* right from wrong.

Furthermore there seems to be little to suggest that our pupils have no conception that certain acts can be morally unacceptable. They certainly talk as if they believe some things are wrong and they complain eloquently when they think they are the victims of wrong-doing. The problem may be, not that they have no ideas about what is right and wrong, but that their ideas do not always concur with those of others.

When there is talk of children having little or no sense of morality, 'morality' is often intended to signify that which is morally right (or rather what the complainant *deems* to be morally right). In other words, the implication is that children lack a proper understanding of morality in that their ideas of right and wrong are mistaken. However, 'morality' might also refer to the sphere of morality (to the whole area which concerns what is morally good or bad rather than, for example, what is aesthetically good or bad) so that the fear expressed is that young people's moral sensibility is undesirably diminished or limited, such that moral considerations are not always recognized or acted upon. The force of expediency, self-interest and instrumental arguments may be thought to take precedence over, or to obliterate, reflection on moral factors in some situations. While conceding that murder is readily identified as a moral matter, there may be anxiety that practices such as tax-dodging are not perceived as moral issues, but as socially acceptable – what everyone would do if they could get away with it. The worry may be that 'What ought I to do?' is being ignored in the face of 'What can I be expected to do?' Thus the young are perceived as less discriminating and less scrupulous than is desirable.

It is also possible that some are concerned that the nature of morality is misunderstood in other ways, and that young people's commitment to moral values is eroded by unreflective adherence to a relativist or subjectivist position. After all, they might say, one does not need to engage in sophisticated, philosophical thought to gain the impression that moral values are primarily cultural, relative to time and place, or to conclude they are just a matter of taste. A lack of certainty, and a consequent *laissez-faire* attitude with respect to what is right or wrong may well be feared.

How far these implicit assumptions or the fears which ride on them are well grounded is, of course, highly debatable; but even if they were justifiable it is a further question whether or not *teachers* must teach children what is right and wrong. The issues raised already intimate that the answer is likely to depend a great deal on what exactly is meant by this, but some clarification can be achieved by concentrating initially on the notion of moral education.

MORAL EDUCATION

If education is under consideration, the aim cannot be merely to train pupils, as if they are dogs or parrots, to act in certain ways. There can be little doubt that many people would very much like teachers to concentrate on producing young adults whose conduct conforms to that which is deemed to be desirable, law-abiding and morally acceptable. But education concerns more than trained behaviour: education concerns teaching with regard for children's capacity to understand, know and reason. Moral education, and any other education, must involve cognition and should not be reduced to training or conditioning behaviour. Equally, with respect to beliefs, moral education is not reducible to indoctrination or to the inculcation of moral values such that children are brought to believe certain actions are morally right or wrong just because teachers say so:

> ...there are rational considerations. As a matter of rationality, there are moral claims which we have to recognise. But we have to recognise them, rather than blindly following answers given by others. If something like this is right, then the idea of imposing morality on others becomes a contradiction in terms. People will have to appreciate the force of moral thinking for themselves, and there will be a role for moral education, not in imposing anything, but rather in enabling people to see what in the end they will have to see for themselves. (Haydon 1997, p. 84)

Moral education is surely intended to help children to be able to think and act morally – to develop as moral agents. Despite some doubts over what might be meant by 'moral development' (see White 1994), moral education must at least be about developing those capacities needed to function in the moral sphere. Being moral is not a matter of blind obedience to others, or doing the right thing for fear of reprisals; it requires that people act autonomously, freely acting in the light of beliefs which in some significant sense they have made their own.

If teaching what is right and wrong amounts to coercing or manipulating pupils into unthinking conformity, then it is clear that this is not the task of schools. If, on the other hand, it means enabling children to be full moral agents, building on what they already understand of moral concepts – right and wrong, good and bad – this is surely at the heart of moral education.

It must be absurd to imagine that secondary school students have no moral beliefs at all, but believing something to be morally wrong is not the same as understanding the moral sphere itself. One of the first concerns for moral education surely should be to address the nature of moral beliefs as such.

THE NATURE OF MORALITY

Moral beliefs are not the same in kind as beliefs about scientific or mathematical propositions. Morals are not facts or knowledge that can be arrived at simply by assessing empirical evidence or pursuing logical argument. Questions of morality are questions about what is right and wrong, about what people ought to do, not just about what is the case. Answering moral questions involves making judgements in the light of principles held and moral values perceived. Facts and reasoning are not irrelevant, but, in the final analysis, morals are unverifiable and are the proper object of belief rather than knowledge. It cannot be proved beyond doubt that it is wrong to torture, in the way that the correct height of a tree can be established. Evidence and reason are important in showing that torturers inflict agony, but it is the belief that we should not unjustifiably inflict pain which is crucial in deciding whether or not torture is morally acceptable, and not the fact that torture is still widely used in some prisons. We *believe* rather than *know* that some acts are wrong.

To say that morals are not reducible to facts is not to say they are exclusively subjective or merely arbitrary, nor is it to suggest that all beliefs about morality are equally valid. Moral beliefs based on misapprehension of the relevant facts, on incoherent reasoning or chosen at random are evidently less defensible than judgements arrived at through coherent reasoning and taking into account relevant evidence. Yes, moral education aims to help children to hold moral values they have chosen for themselves, but this should not be thought of as some trivial 'pick 'n' mix' process, reflecting mere taste or whim.

Moral beliefs are *controversial* in their nature and open to question in the sense explained by Terry McLaughlin in Chapter 11. They are *values*. At the same time, moral values are distinct from other values such as aesthetic, political and intellectual values. That which is believed to be morally acceptable may coincide with or overlap the law, social mores, cultural traditions and religious beliefs, but is also distinguishable from these. We may derive the particular moral beliefs we hold from, for example, religious teaching or what society approves, but morals are also separable. What we believe to be morally right may at times contradict the law of the land or conflict with a particular religious tenet. In judging an action to be morally good or bad, relying on convention and conviction will be inadequate: 'That a principle is backed by tradition, intuition, power or revelation does not make it a moral principle. Only if it is rationally justifiable is it that' (Hirst 1973, p. 140). Moral considerations are generally held to be over-riding; transcending social conventions, expediency and other values.

Morality is controversial in its logical status, but is also the subject of controversy in the ordinary sense. People vary in their specific moral beliefs and disagree over what is morally right or wrong. Understanding the moral sphere includes appreciation of the diversity of moral values, of different conceptions of right and wrong.

If moral values are so varied and uncertain, it may seem that we should not be attempting to teach right and wrong since cultural relativism may appear to be the only appropriate stance in a pluralist society. But diversity does not *have* to entail thoroughgoing cultural relativism or equal acceptance of irreconcilable views.

Nevertheless, given the evident diversity, it is clear that moral education is a sensitive matter. Our moral values are usually important to us. A value is something held in high esteem, something dear to us, and in addition our moral beliefs are part of who we are and a reflection of our ideals. Consequently arguments about what is morally right or wrong are not only likely to be intransigent, they may also often be heated.

CAN ANY MORAL VALUES LEGITIMATELY BE TAUGHT?

Whose moral values?

The potential for conflicting views on what is morally acceptable and what is not, between parents and schools or between teachers and children, is plain. Who is to decide which moral values should be promoted in schools? While there are no good grounds for accepting that teachers are the only proper arbiters of what is right and good, by the same token parents and others do not always know better. Troublesome clashes are unlikely to be avoided by passing the decision-making over to parents who may disagree among themselves – or to another body.

There are no moral experts to whom we can apply for *information* about what is right and wrong or what the content of moral education ought to be. Some people may be better than others at making moral judgements; nevertheless, such people do not form a class comparable to other sets of experts, to whom we might apply to make certain judgements for us. Even a degree in moral philosophy would not necessarily signal the specific expertise required. Undoubtedly training in moral philosophy would be useful in clarifying and analysing the nature of particular ethical dilemmas, but more is needed. The expertise required includes practical wisdom and being a good person, and there is little reason to suppose that moral philosophers are morally better *persons* than others.

Far more importantly, even if there were an identifiable set of moral experts, the notion of leaving decisions about what is right or wrong to them would remain unacceptable – morally unacceptable. To rely on the moral understanding of others and to surrender one's choice of moral action in unreflectingly accepting their advice, would be to relinquish part of being a person. A person thinks and acts morally in virtue of doing so with some relevant *autonomy*. In simply conforming to the ideas of the expert, one has abdicated from making further moral choices with respect to their sphere of enquiry and cannot properly be said to think or act morally in any consequent conformity. (This is not to suggest that no expert judgement is ever relevant to making moral decisions, but to maintain that mere conformity to another's advice cannot be autonomous thought or action. It is of course distinct from applying to experts for their specialized *knowledge* of a particular area and relying on their authority in their own fields, or taking their views into account in arriving at one's own decision.) We may not be all equally qualified for or good at making moral judgements, but to permit others to decide for us is to stop being moral at all. We need to achieve more expertise ourselves and to acquire the disposition to act in the light of it, not to leave it to others.

Should moral education be only about morality?

It might be thought therefore that schools should concentrate on teaching *about* morality and avoid any attempt to teach what is right or wrong in any more direct sense. But refraining from exerting any influence over pupils' moral beliefs does not seem to be an option that is, in practice, open to teachers. It is easy to recognize that the hidden curriculum, in the sense of all that is implicit in the way teachers present lessons and treat their pupils, is full of messages about what they value and believe with respect to morality. Moreover, this implicit curriculum may be highly influential. It may be that we arrive at many of our moral convictions from the example of others and from how we are treated, rather than from direct instruction or discussion.

Thus it must be important to reflect on what, if any, moral values can be legitimately taught, and to confront the issue explicitly in moral education.

Fundamental and specific moral beliefs

The 1996 School Curriculum and Assessment Authority consultative document on values education was part of a process seeking to identify those values which are shared and should be promoted in schools in England and Wales. SCAA made explicit that the statements of value agreed upon were not intended to be 'a definitive and complete list of all the values people hold' (National Forum for Values in Education and the Community 1996, p. 1); moreover, it was emphasized that:

> the shared values will not necessarily be the values that all people believe to be the most important. By their nature, for example, 'shared values' do not include those distinctive of any particular religious or cultural group (*ibid*. 1996, p. 5).

Evidently the values sought are those on which agreement seems possible and indeed likely. There is no claim that such values are the objects of universal consensus, only that there may be agreement on values that 'schools should promote on society's behalf' (*ibid*. 1996, Introduction).

A MORI 'omnibus' poll of 1,500 adults apparently showed that 95 per cent of those consulted were agreed on the values put forward in the statement: 'This overwhelming consensus is empirical evidence for the claim that, despite the fact that we are a pluralist society, there is a robust set of values that are shared by all of us' (Talbot and Tate 1997, p. 3). The fact that there may be wide agreement or even consensus with regard to moral or any other values cannot, however, alone justify their inclusion in the school curriculum. While broad agreement might well in practical terms facilitate the teacher's task, for example by helping to avoid conflicts with parents and others, it could not *justify* the intentional promotion of particular moral values in school. Other grounds are needed.

However, it may be that there is wide agreement on certain moral values, not purely as a matter of coincidence, but because in some way they are fundamental. It may be the case that these are readily shared values, not because contingently there is agreement about them, but because without appreciating them it is difficult to see how one could understand what it is to be a moral agent.

Some values seem to be fundamental to understanding morality itself. The SCAA Statement of Values includes:

> We value truth, human rights, the law, justice and the collective endeavour for the common good of society. (National Forum for Values in Education and the Community 1996, p. 2)

> We value others for themselves, not for what they have or what they can do for us. (*ibid.*, p. 2)

> We value each person as a unique being of intrinsic worth. (*ibid.* p. 3)

Valuing others 'for themselves' appears to be fundamental to understanding what it is to be moral. In other words, it is difficult to imagine how one could begin to act and think as a moral agent without appreciating the value of respect for persons. In the same way, notions such as impartiality, justice and truth are also held to be basic to moral agency:

> ... treating other people with respect, not causing unnecessary hurt or pain, taking seriously other people's interests, telling the truth and keeping promises. It is difficult to conceive a morality that did not subscribe in some way to such principles. (Pring 1987, p. 65)

If such concepts are fundamental to functioning morally, it must be legitimate, and indeed necessary, to promote them in moral education.

A distinction can be drawn between such *fundamental values* and *specific moral beliefs*. Fundamental values do seem to be in a different category from specific beliefs. The principle that human life should be respected is fundamental, but a range of differing specific beliefs might follow from this. Whether or not respect for life demands a stand which is pacifist, anti-abortion or anti-euthanasia is contentious. Pacifism comprises a specific instance of respect for life, but is not the only defensible position to take on war. Accepting others for themselves is significantly different from believing that this must be reflected in generous donations to charity.

In pluralistic societies such as our own, consensus that specific moral beliefs are right must be unlikely, perhaps because beliefs in this category are inherently so contestable. But it is important to note that fundamental values too are not incontrovertible or uncontentious. In this respect they are no different from many specific moral beliefs. To value everyone as having intrinsic worth may be basic to moral thinking, but it is not morally neutral or incontestable (cf Cohen 1969, p. 160).

Promoting or teaching *specific* values will always be educationally dubious, but it may be entirely appropriate to foster a concern for *fundamental* values in moral education. This will involve nurturing and refining the understanding that certain concepts are central to morality.

EDUCATING FOR MORAL AGENCY

To develop as a moral agent involves more than intellectual comprehension of the moral sphere and coming to appreciate certain fundamental values:

> children may be taught a great deal about morality without being taught to be moral agents; they may fail to use the information and the skills they have acquired, when faced with a real-life moral decision, or they may fail to act upon the moral judgements they have formed. (Straughan 1982, p. 90)

Children do need to be able to act morally as well as to think, to be taught 'that right and wrong are real and applicable, not merely verbal distinctions' (Warnock 1996, p. 49). Moral education which aimed to have no bearing on behaviour would surely be extraordinary. There should in this regard, however, be no suggestion that schools ought to engage in behavioural conditioning or non-educative practices designed to regulate conduct, not only because this would be unduly manipulatory, but also because moral action cannot be completely divorced from intellectual processes. Acting morally is not always to act spontaneously, on whim or at random. A measure of rationality needs to be cultivated if people are to make decisions about what they ought to do and to act on them; but in addition, moral agents are those who have a sense of obligation to follow their own principles and the disposition to do so.

Moral principles are beliefs or values in the light of which the moral agent makes judgements and decides how to act. They can be seen as rules or guidelines to which a person feels committed. Moral education involves the cultivation of dispositions: not necessarily the disposition to perform a specific action such as joining a protest march, but at least the disposition to act in accordance with one's principles rather than ignoring them. This is not to say that morally educated persons will always behave according to their moral beliefs or in ways which conform to their consciences, but moral agents will be aware when they have acted rightly or wrongly. In this sense moral agents know right from wrong.

Spiecker would also want moral education to include attention to moral emotions and attitudes, pointing out that: 'Educators not only try to teach children to act according to moral rules . . . they also want them to do so with "heart and soul" and "in the right spirit"' (Spiecker 1988, p. 53).

Whether they are best described as emotions and attitudes or in different terms, the affective aspects of morality cannot be ignored. It must be possible to lead a morally blameless life and even to perform good deeds out of a strong sense of duty without feeling empathy with other human beings; but, for many of us, understanding what we ought to do springs from feeling for others, and our sense of moral obligation is strong because we feel inclined to be altruistic, kindly, fair or whatever. Our feelings contribute to our motivation to act in certain ways. Moreover, a range of emotions are *appropriately* experienced by moral agents; for example, it is appropriate to feel ashamed when we think we have done wrong. Feelings too may need to be recognized, understood and encouraged in moral education.

Trying to conduct one's life in the light of one's moral principles may also require resolution or strength of will, so moral education may need to include empowerment – raising and maintaining pupils' self-esteem and developing their assertiveness, as well as providing knowledge and understanding – in order to help young people to adhere to their principles in the face of opposition and to stand up for what they feel to be morally right.

MORAL DEVELOPMENT

The Education Reform Act 1988 states in its first requirement that the curriculum should promote 'the spiritual, moral, cultural, mental and physical development of pupils'. Schools, then, are *expected* to educate for moral *development*.

Kohlberg's research (1966, 1969) led him to conclude that there is a pattern to moral development, and that there are consecutive levels and stages through which children and young adults pass. His work focused closely on children's moral *reasoning*. His developmental scheme can be briefly summarized as shown in Figure 12.1 (for further details see Pring 1987, pp. 40ff).

If a developmental view is adopted, presumably moral education should, in terms of this model, aim to help pupils to move towards Stage 6 (although Kohlberg believed that few adults actually achieve this level of sophistication in their moral reasoning). This would involve enabling and encouraging children to move from heteronomy and being led by self-interest to recognition of the claims of others and eventually to being guided by concern for others and impartiality. In the context of education, such a focus on the development of moral reasoning seems entirely appropriate and desirable. It would, however, be foolish to suppose that an intellectual grasp of sophisticated reasoning will, of itself, preclude anti-social behaviour. As Wringe wryly notes: 'it is unlikely that the young mugger or joy-rider will have asked herself "Can I will the maxim of this act to become a universal law?" and simply hit upon the wrong answer' (Wringe 1998, p. 226).

Developing moral judgement and improving moral reasoning are thus vital to moral development, but moral education cannot be confined to this if it is to affect moral action.

| LEVEL 1 |
| Pre-conventional |

| Stage1 |
| Heteronomous morality |

| Stage 2 |
| Instrumentalism |

| LEVEL 2 |
| Conventional |

| Stage 3 |
| Interpersonal and conformist |

| Stage 4 |
| Social system maintenance |

| LEVEL 3 |
| Post-conventional |

| Stage 5 |
| Social contract, rights |

| Stage 6 |
| Universal ethical principles |

Figure 12.1: Kohlberg's developmental scheme

Chapter 13

Citizenship and Education for Citizenship

JOHN BECK

THE DEVELOPMENT OF CITIZENSHIP EDUCATION IN BRITAIN

In Britain, compared with many other nations, explicit education for citizenship has been relatively neglected.[1] At certain moments of crisis, efforts have been made to promote it, a case in point being the formation of the Association for Education in World Citizenship which was established in 1935 in response to the perceived threat to democracy posed by the rise of both Communism and Fascism. Similar concerns – to educate for democracy as a safeguard against a recurrence of totalitarian politics – motivated a brief period of enthusiasm for citizenship education in Britain in the post-war years. Significantly however, the Ministry of Education was equivocal in its support for these developments (Ministry of Education 1949) and gave no national lead. From the mid-1960s, the growth of comprehensive schooling helped provide an impetus for a major expansion of education in the general area of the social studies – with new GCE and CSE syllabuses in subjects like Politics, Sociology, Social Studies, Integrated Humanities, as well as the growth of General Studies in sixth forms. But even then, such subjects were typically offered only as options and there was little support for *universal* citizenship education.

The introduction of the National Curriculum in 1988 saw the first effort to include citizenship as a required element in the education of all young people in England and Wales. This, however, took the form of introducing education for citizenship as one of no fewer than five 'cross-curricular themes' which schools were supposed to include in their curricula alongside the statutorily prescribed and assessed Core, Foundation and Basic subjects. (See National Curriculum Council 1990; also, for an outline of these cross-curricular initiatives see Fogelman 1997; and for a critique, Beck 1998, Ch. 5). In the event, the sheer weight of the statutory elements meant that few schools had either the time or energy to pay much attention to citizenship education. Not only this, but many teachers complained that their efforts were further hampered by a lack of clarity about the meaning and content of this area of the curriculum. For example, a comprehensive school headteacher, addressing an audience of PGCE 'trainees' in Cambridge in 1995, commented:

> Of the five cross-curriculum 'themes' of the National Curriculum, we have taken on four more or less full-frontal. As for the other one – when someone tells us what education for citizenship is, I'm sure that will trigger a response. (Quoted in Beck 1998, p. 96)

Although this reaction was perhaps a little uncharitable in view of the efforts of several national agencies which were by then actively promoting citizenship education in schools (e.g. the Citizenship Foundation, the Centre for Citizenship Studies), there are, as we shall see, good reasons why it is difficult to offer definitions of citizenship which are not only succinct and accurate but which also provide clear guidance about how schools should educate for citizenship.

A decade after the introduction of the National Curriculum, a further effort to promote citizenship education was initiated. This took the form of the establishment by the Secretary of State for Education and Employment of an Advisory Group on Citizenship, whose remit was to provide:

> advice on effective education for citizenship in schools, to include the nature and practices of participation in democracy; the duties, responsibilities and rights of individuals as citizens; and the value to individuals and society of community activity.

This group, chaired by Professor Bernard Crick, published its Final Report in September 1998 (Advisory Group on Citizenship 1998). The Report set out an ambitious programme of 'essential elements of citizenship education' and recommended that not less than five per cent of the total curriculum should be devoted to it across the 5–16 age range.

At about the same time as Crick's group was presenting its conclusions, no fewer than four other official advisory groups were working on further reports – on a range of issues all directly or indirectly relevant to citizenship. These included: The Advisory Group on Sustainable Development; The National Advisory Group for Personal, Social and Health Education; The National Advisory Committee on Creative and Cultural Education; and the QCA's Project for Spiritual, Moral, Social and Cultural Development. Faced with this array of partially overlapping and partially competing pressures for scarce curriculum time, the QCA established its own Preparation for Adult Life working party, charged with the task of trying to synthesize and reconcile the proposals emanating from all these groups, with a view to advising ministers as they considered revisions to the National Curriculum to take effect from the year 2000. In May 1999, the QCA published a consultation document containing the Secretary of State's proposals for the revised National Curriculum to be introduced from September 2000 onwards (QCA/DfEE 1999). The document contained proposals not only for a non-statutory framework for PSHE and citizenship education across all four Key Stages of the National Curriculum but also 'draft programmes of study and an attainment target for a proposed new Foundation Subject for citizenship at Key Stages 3 and 4' (*ibid.*, p. 28). Broadly following the recommendations of Crick's Advisory Group, the draft statutory order provided guidance in the form of a relatively 'light touch' approach, based upon a framework of quite broad learning outcomes, with schools being given considerable latitude in deciding on both the specifics of content and on how citizenship education would be delivered. The proposals did, nevertheless, contain clear directions about content areas – for example, indicating that at Key Stage 4:

> pupils should be taught about ... the work of parliament, the govern-ment and the courts; ... the significance of active participation in democratic and electoral processes; ... the importance of a free press and the role of the media; ... the rights and responsibilities of con-sumers, employers and employees ... (*ibid.*, p. 31)

Many of the ideas from the other advisory groups were also endorsed in the QCA document taken as a whole – but citizenship was clearly prioritized.

WHAT IS CITIZENSHIP?

As has already been suggested, one reason for the neglect of citizenship edu-cation in Britain has been the lack of clarity about the nature of citizenship itself. Clearly, a society cannot *educate* for citizenship unless there exists a rea-sonably explicit and consensual conception of what the key characteristics of citizenship are. Some commentators have seen relatively little problem here. For example, the authors of the House of Commons Commission on Citizen-ship 1990 confidently suggested that it was possible to broadly identify what they called 'the British approach to citizenship' (Commission on Citizenship 1990, p. 4). This essentially involved endorsing the conception of citizenship set out by T. H. Marshall in his influential book *Citizenship and Social Class* which was published in 1950.

T. H. Marshall's conception of citizenship

Marshall told a persuasive story about the nature of citizenship and its histor-ical development. The book is what some would now call a 'grand narrative' – a story of moral and political progress, an account of a long march towards increasing enlightenment. Marshall argued that, at least as it had developed in Britain, citizenship mainly emerged over three successive centuries, each of which saw the growth of a different 'element' of citizenship. Each of these elements involved the extension of different kinds of *rights* to individuals: rights which provided important kinds of *protection* for the individual. These were chiefly defences against the exercise of arbitrary or unaccountable power, and against adverse economic and personal circumstances.

The 'civic' element/civic rights

According to Marshall, these developed mainly in the eighteenth century. This element included a range of legal rights and protections, the most important of which were:

- The establishment of the rule of law and the principle of equality before the law so that even the most powerful individuals and institutions (including the state) were subject to the rule of law.[2]
- Freedom of conscience ('freedom of speech, thought and faith' as Marshall himself put it).
- Freedom to own property, to transmit it to one's heirs, to enter into legally binding contracts, etc.

The 'political' element/political rights

In Britain, political rights were achieved mainly in the nineteenth century – though we do well to remember that many of these rights were not won by women until well into the twentieth century. This element primarily involved those democratic political liberties which enable all adult citizens to have some influence over the laws by which they are governed. As Ralph Dahrendorf has put it: 'unless all citizens have an opportunity to feed their interests into the law, the rule of law leaves serious inequalities of entitlement. That is why political rights were necessary to supplement civil rights' (Dahrendorf 1996, p. 38).

The key political rights include:

- Freedom of expression and freedom of association (e.g. press freedom, the right to belong to political parties, trade unions, pressure groups, etc.).
- The extension of the franchise (eventually to all adult men and women) – this involved voting in relation to forms of representative rather than participatory democratic politics.
- Rights for eligible citizens to participate in the governance of smaller-scale institutions within 'civil society' – e.g. school governing bodies, National Health Service Trusts, as well as a whole range of voluntary associations.

Of course, the desirable *extent* of such rights remains contested in many respects: relevant current examples include employees' claims to be represented in the boardroom, or student representation on management committees in higher education.

The 'social' element/social rights

The most novel and most controversial of Marshall's three elements of citizenship was what he called the social element. Marshall wanted to extend the concept of citizenship to include a set of entitlements which would protect individuals from certain risks which are inseparable from the operation of market forces within capitalist economies. The key risk was that of being plunged into poverty as a result of unemployment, ill health, old age, etc. – i.e. risks associated with being unable to support oneself by one's own labour in a 'free' economy. To put it differently, he was concerned with what he saw as the real 'unfreedoms' which the free play of market forces entailed for some people at key points in their lives. He therefore proposed that the ideal of citizenship should be extended to include a basic entitlement to *welfare:* 'the right to a modicum of economic welfare and security'. What was novel about Marshall's position was not, of course, the notion of welfare benefits as such, but the claim that access to a certain minimum of such benefits should be a *full right of citizenship.* As Marshall himself unambiguously put it, the social element of citizenship involved 'a universal right to a real income not proportionate to the market value of the claimant' (*ibid.,* p. 39). Similarly, he proposed, citizens should have rights to certain minimum levels of free education and health care.

Marshall advanced three key arguments in support of social citizenship. The first was that these minimum social entitlements were a precondition of individuals being able effectively to exercise their other rights of citizenship. Chronic ill health, poverty, a rudimentary level of education, etc., all prevented individuals from functioning as full citizens. Second, he argued that there was a need in modern and affluent Western democracies, to balance the amoral logic of capitalist economic production and the severe social inequalities it generated, with the moral or 'normative' logic which he felt was inherent in the historical development of the citizenship ideal. This normative logic, based upon principles of equality and social justice, pointed to the progressive extension of welfare provision as an entitlement. Citizenship, he said: 'is an urge towards a fuller measure of equality, an enrichment of the stuff of which the status (of citizen) is made, and an increase in the number on whom that status is bestowed' (Marshall 1964, p. 92). The third reason Marshall advocated social citizenship had to do with social integration. Citizenship, he argued, could be a 'common possession', a common status which conferred dignity on all members of society. In this way, it counterbalanced the potentially divisive inequalities of social class – and thus operated as a principle of social solidarity.

Challenges to social citizenship: Conservative 'active citizenship'

Marshall's ideas had considerable resonance and plausibility in Britain in the decades following the Second World War – and also in several other contemporary Western European societies which saw a similar extension of state welfare provision. This expansion of 'the welfare state' coincided with a period during which most Western European economies enjoyed a so-called 'long boom' of continuously rising prosperity and full employment. Under these economic conditions, political parties of both left and right fell under the spell of what has been termed 'consensus politics' – meaning that the main political parties, albeit with varying degrees of enthusiasm, promoted the expansion of the state's role in the provision of welfare and social security. In Britain, this period of consensus came to an end in the mid-1970s, when the country's economic weakness was exposed by a period of severe recession triggered by a 400 per cent increase in the world oil price. This, as well as other more fundamental tensions associated with rising inflation and problems of controlling levels of public spending, helped to promote a process of political reassessment and polarization, in which Conservative thinking shifted markedly to the right, while certain sections of the Labour Party moved leftward. Margaret Thatcher's election victory in 1979 both symbolized and consolidated the victory of these more right-wing doctrines – notably policies aiming to 'roll back' the state, to curtail the power of trade unions and the professions, and to embrace market forces in the provision of welfare services, including education and health.

Under these changed conditions, conceptions of citizenship of a more Conservative stamp began to be articulated with increasing confidence. As Ralph Dahrendorf has pointed out, Marshallian notions of social citizenship had never taken root in the USA, where a much more abrasive conception of the scope of the protections to which individual citizens were entitled was never displaced:

> Civil rights, political rights and the open frontier summed up the American concept of liberty. To some extent they still do. The poor deserve help if they help themselves; otherwise their condition is their own affair. (*op. cit.*, pp. 38–9)

Throughout the 1980s and into the 90s, the New Right, mainly in the USA and the UK, articulated an increasingly influential critique of welfarism. This critique claimed that notions of welfare rights had engendered a 'dependency culture' which took away the incentive for individuals to strive to seek work to support themselves and their dependants, that welfarism had undermined self-respect and moral fibre, that this had undermined family values, for example by offering guaranteed state support for single mothers and their offspring; and finally, that the productive members of society were being unfairly taxed to support the unproductive. The poorer sections of society needed to be compelled to 'price themselves back into jobs' – i.e. to accept work at 'realistic' levels of pay determined by market forces. The idea of social *rights* as rights of citizenship was bogus. What needed emphasizing instead were the *duties* of individuals to be law-abiding, to be socially responsible, and to make economic provision for themselves and their dependants.

Alongside this tough-minded economic individualism, sections of the right also advocated a notion of 'active citizenship'. In part, this was addressed to the more privileged sections of society – reminding them that the self-interest of those who were economically successful needed to be tempered by an ethic of 'contribution' to the wider good of the 'community'. Crucially, this conception of active citizenship centred in the idea of voluntary commitment rather than – and indeed in place of – state provision. The Conservative minister Douglas Hurd was a leading advocate of this kind of active citizenship. He sought to link it not only to 'Victorian values' of self-help, thrift, and hard work, but also to traditions of voluntary service which, he asserted, were more authentically British than the doctrines of socialist intellectuals:

> The Conservative Party is moving forward from its justified concern with the motor of wealth creation towards a redefinition of how the individual citizen, business, or voluntary group can use resources and leisure to help the community . . . The English tradition of voluntary service is, of course, not new . . . What *is* new is the rediscovery that schemes based on this tradition are often more flexible and more effective than bureaucratic plans drawn up on the Fabian principle . . . A social policy founded upon ideals of responsible and active citizenship is compatible with free market economic policies. (Hurd 1988)

New Labour and citizenship

Although it is too early to judge accurately, the repertoire of ideas and policies emanating from New Labour in Britain could be interpreted as an attempt to combine elements of both of these approaches to citizenship. On the one hand, policies to combat 'social exclusion', the reintroduction of some elements of redistributive taxation (redistributing income from richer to poorer), the explicit commitment to the National Health Service and state education, etc. could all be read as indications of support for Marshallian conceptions of social citizenship. However, other elements of New Labour's repertoire draw quite explicitly on the inheritance of New Right thinking – for example: the explicit support for 'enterprise culture' as the key to wealth creation, the enthusiasm for 'meritocracy', the moralistic denunciation of 'dependency culture' and the associated tendency to selectively penalize the 'undeserving poor'.

One danger inherent in New Labour's approach is that its much vaunted 'Third Way' *can* be represented as an irreversible progression 'beyond ideology' into a new world that has left behind the 'anachronistic' polarities of left and right. Within such a framework of assumptions, there could lurk a facile but plausible conception that we can now simply educate for the majority consensual view – and that this is what education for citizenship should be mainly about: a civic education congenial to 'middle England'! The key risk here is that of seeming to have abolished value choices. Although there is no inevitability that political values in any society will remain polarized, let alone polarized along the axis of traditional left-v.-right divisions, it is nevertheless also true that it is not possible to move 'beyond ideology' in the sense that *no* value judgements underlie our way of life or social arrangements. Citizenship is and will always remain a *contested* concept, at least in the sense that alternative and competing conceptions will always be available. As David Hogan has recently reminded us, it was no less an authority than Aristotle who declared in *The Politics* that citizenship is a matter about which 'there is no unanimity of agreement' (Aristotle 1981, p. 168; Hogan 1997, p. 51).

CITIZENSHIP AND VALUE DIVERSITY IN PLURALISTIC SOCIETIES

It is precisely the issue of value diversity in modern societies, and the problems that such diversity may pose in relation to social cohesion, that has recently become another key focus of debate among writers interested in citizenship.

Modern liberal democracies are highly *pluralistic* in a number of respects:

- The legacy of colonialism and the effects of mass migration have brought about increased ethnic diversity and the greater cultural diversity that goes with it; this often includes the co-existence of several different religious faith communities within a single society.
- In some societies (as in North and South America) which were settled by Europeans and subsequently became independent nations, there are communities of indigenous peoples in addition to the diversity produced by successive waves of immigration as well as the legacy of slavery.
- The effects of 'globalization', in both its economic and cultural aspects, are deeply invasive of localized and traditional ways of life: to an unprecedented extent, people across the world have no alternative but to become aware of alternative ways of life, alternative values, alternative beliefs.

All these developments create a situation in which not only individuals but communities – sometimes with very different outlooks and values – must co-exist within the framework of a single polity and society.

However, these developments do not exhaust the sources of value diversity. Perhaps even more significant is the steady advance in modern societies of those rationalistic and scientific forms of knowledge and understanding of ourselves and of the world, which are sometimes described as Western. It is this *knowledge* which is one of the key sources of the 'openness' which 'Western' democratic societies exhibit. An open society is, perhaps above all else, one that permits (and even encourages) wide-ranging rational interrogation of claims to the possession of truth – however authoritative the source of such claims. Such sceptical, critical reason is, however, profoundly corrosive of what Descartes called 'custom and example'. It tends to undermine established 'certainties', to de-throne religious and other dogmas, and to encourage ordinary people as well as philosophers and scientists to ask 'Why?' – and to enter into public debate about existing social arrangements and cultural assumptions. In Ernest Gellner's words: 'there are no privileged knowers, no organisation is allowed to claim cognitive monopoly, there are no privileged events or objects. Logical cogency and evidence are king' (Gellner 1992, p. 146).

Much recent debate in liberal political theory has focused upon the question of how social integration and the stability of liberal political systems can be maintained in the face of this increasing diversity of beliefs and values, as well as the increased *consciousness* of such diversity that is such a feature of modern life. In a certain sense, liberal politics is itself part of the problem here. After all, the Western tradition of citizenship has been essentially what David Hogan, in an illuminating phrase, has termed a tradition of 'protective citizenship' (Hogan 1997).[3] It is a politics built around discourses of *rights* – most significantly rights protecting the legitimate freedoms of individuals and groups from unwarranted interference by others, whether from more powerful fellow citizens, dominant social groups, or the state itself. Historically, freedom of *religious* belief was a key issue around which struggles to achieve such protection were fought out. The point of these struggles was precisely to establish protected freedom of conscience as well as the right to worship as individual conscience dictated. In other words, what was being fought for was the *right* to be a 'dissenter' or 'Protestant' in relation to the previously prevailing conceptions of truth upheld by the established Church. The eventual victory of dissenters in these respects was an early and key step in the protection of pluralism.

A fundamental problem for liberal politics and liberal conceptions of citizenship, therefore, is this: how far and in what ways is a liberal democratic state justified in infringing the freedoms of individuals and groups? Perhaps the first point to notice here is that 'democracy' *per se* does not provide anything like a complete answer. Superficially, it might seem that once a democratic system of government has been established, then decisions taken by the elected political representatives of the majority are *ipso facto* legitimate, and that is the end of the matter. But a moment's reflection reveals a basic problem with this simplistic view. This is that it can result in quite unacceptable forms of 'majoritarianism' – the tyranny of the majority over minorities. (This has, of course, been a potent cause of chronic social division between majorities and minorities in areas such as Northern Ireland and the former Yugoslavia, to mention only two topical and tragic instances.) Majoritarianism of such kinds is clearly incompatible with certain fundamental principles of protective liberal citizenship – notably the recognition of the rights of individuals to be self-determining so long as their actions are not demonstrably harmful to others. A genuinely liberal interpretation of democracy, therefore, must have built into it principles and mechanisms to protect the autonomy, interests and ways of life of legitimate minorities.

But recognizing this still leaves a great deal of room for reasoned debate about the extent to which, and the respects in which, it is justifiable for governments in liberal democracies to interfere in and restrict the freedoms of their citizens. There is little argument that in most circumstances the state is entitled to prohibit and 'police' actions that are demonstrably injurious to others and/or to society as a whole. Prohibition of murder, rape, domestic violence against women or children, drunk-driving, burglary, etc. are all obvious examples. But a feature of liberal pluralism is that individuals and groups are attached to very significantly different conceptions of the 'good life'. And their attachment to these different 'comprehensive theories of the good' as the philosopher John Rawls calls them (Rawls 1993), can result in deep differences of belief about, say, the acceptability of homosexuality or of abortion, about when it is legitimate to engage in warfare, or whether within certain communities it is legitimate to limit women's liberties if women themselves in these communities accept such restrictions, etc. Once such differences are recognized, a further set of problems arises relating to the question of how such liberal societies should educate their future citizens. For example, should parents, by virtue of *being* parents, be free to bring up their children in conformity with their own beliefs and values and to insulate them as far as possible from competing viewpoints? Or, alternatively, is the state justified in intervening so as to try to ensure that the education of all young people introduces a wide-ranging examination of competing arguments and evidence about matters which are, in the society as a whole, controversial? An underlying question here concerns the extent to which a liberal society has a duty to promote ethical autonomy as well as political autonomy in young people. (Democratic liberal institutions, after all, presuppose an ideal of political autonomy: reasoned public deliberation about complex and controversial issues is the very stuff of political argument and decision-making in a democracy.) These questions are also related to the scope of the sphere of 'public values' in relation to 'non-public' values – an issue which is discussed in more detail in Chapter 11.[4]

CONCLUSION

In a brief introductory discussion such as this, it is not possible to discuss the different positions within these debates in any detail. However, what may be worthwhile in conclusion, is to highlight just how wide is the range of responses that now exists to the shared recognition of the highly pluralistic character of contemporary societies. Three such 'responses' to pluralism will be very briefly outlined.

1. Liberal theorists of protective citizenship

Writers of this persuasion tend to support, albeit with significant modifications, John Rawls' idea that the stability of liberal polities in the face of extensive value pluralism is most likely to be sustained by serious efforts on the part of all citizens of goodwill to reason together to construct an 'overlapping consensus' on common public values. Citizens are called upon to seek the common ground between the otherwise very diverse comprehensive theories of the good life to which they are attached. This area of overlap is the sphere of 'public values' which all citizens are seen as having a duty to support. The values in question constitute a kind of minimum basis for the reproduction of a stable liberal polity: they centre on the ideals of justice, of free and equal citizenship, of mutual respect – and the rights and duties derived from these ideals. The overlapping consensus builds support for and thus protects liberal politics itself, as well as the legitimate liberties of citizens. Followers of Rawls disagree with one another about many matters. Perhaps the most significant area of disagreement continues to be the extent to which, and the grounds upon which, the liberal state is justified in restricting the liberties of individual citizens.

2. Communitarian theorists

Most communitarian theorists, albeit for a variety of different reasons, distrust the strong emphasis which liberalism accords to the individual and to the supposed rights of individuals. As Charles Taylor has summarized the situation, there is a continuum of positions here which 'at one end give primacy to individual rights and freedom, and at the other give higher priority to community life and the good of collectivities' (Taylor 1989, pp. 159–60). Politically, communitarians may be inclined to the left or to the right, but all of them tend to think that liberal theories promote an 'excess' of individualism which renders collective life precarious and dangerously weakens people's attachment to the society of which they are part. Communitarians tend to stress the *particularity* of given societies, their shared culture and history, and the need of individuals for a strong and specific cultural grounding of their sense of identity. For these reasons, most communitarians tend to regard the Rawlsian 'overlapping consensus' as something altogether too 'thin' and artificial to command allegiance and commitment, or to function as a viable basis of social solidarity (or even integration). Consequently, most communitarians would support forms of citizenship education which, in David Hogan's words, would 'focus not so much on the protection of individual interests as on social integration and the common good' (Hogan 1997, p. 50). Critics of communitarian positions, however, suggest that communitarians are nostalgic for a premodern world of culturally homogeneous societies, that they have not developed an adequate response to legitimate cultural diversity within any one society, and that their proposals to educate for stronger 'community' values risk becoming indoctrinatory.

3. Postmodernism and citizenship

Postmodernism is even harder to characterize succinctly than protective liberalism or communitarianism – though Gilbert has recently provided a valuable summary which explicity links postmodernism to issues of citizenship (Gilbert 1997). Perhaps the most important of the basic tenets of postmodern thinking is the subversive idea of 'deconstruction'. This includes the claim that 'grand narratives' of ordered progression towards a better future (like Marshall's account of the development of citizenship) are to be radically distrusted. Another candidate for radical deconstruction is the 'integrated self', i.e. the idea that our 'selves' have an ordered coherence and stability, and that we are the authors of our own actions. Postmodernism instead stresses incoherence, discontinuity, and the contradictions that fragment supposedly unitary, cohesive and purposeful wholes. Postmodernism's responses to pluralism are various. One is a tendency to *celebrate* cultural and value diversity, to welcome 'polyculturalism' – not least *because* of the unpredictability of its consequences. Another element of the response is a radical *cultural relativism* which validates the great diversity of previously suppressed cultural 'voices' silenced by various kinds of oppression – the voices of the dispossessed, of women, of indigenous peoples, etc. As far as citizenship is concerned, postmodernists suggest that the preoccupation of most citizenship discourse with the nation state is anachronistic and that it is perceived, especially by the young, as increasingly irrelevant. Postmodernists point instead to the vitality of *other* kinds of politics as constituting new spheres of action which have greater appeal and relevance. These include the 'new social movements' around issues like the environment, transnational concerns with 'human rights', concern about the global power and predatory activities of multinational corporations, etc. Critics of postmodernism, however, highlight what they see as its *own* incoherence: for example its simultaneous celebration of consumerist lifestyles and cultural globalization alongside its enthusiasm for environmentalism. An even deeper source of incoherence, they suggest, lies in the apparent insouciance of some postmodernists about criteria of *truth*. If all 'voices' speak truly because they speak from authentic experience, then when they disagree, are there *any* objective grounds for testing the validity of competing claims? (see Moore and Muller 1999). Postmodernism may have its finger on the pulse of many contemporary developments that are radically changing our lives, but it may also be too loose and incoherent an intellectual framework to offer really satisfactory answers.

NOTES

1. Despite this neglect of explicit civic education within the formally prescribed curriculum, British schools have, nevertheless, been potent agents of broader political socialization. The hierarchical character of the education system, long organized on lines of explicit social class divisions (see Chapter 1), played a key role in perpetuating deep-rooted attitudes of both deference and class antagonism in British political culture. Moreover, for many decades, the teaching of subjects like History and Geography was imbued with strong assumptions about the national and racial superiority of the British, particularly in relation to 'the peoples of the Commonwealth and Empire'. As John Ahier has pointed out in his study of elementary school textbooks in these subjects:

    > ...regional geography ... both established a national confidence and at the same time, a set of assumptions about other races. It located 'them' firmly in their climates and in lands which inhibited their growth towards civilisation

... In the so-called 'hot lands' of the Caribbean and Africa, life was thought to be too easy, there being no necessity to work hard and save ...

In the books, there is a clear implication of a natural hierarchy by which the British are given their place in the world. It is a place that demands hard work and delayed gratification but it offers superiority. (Ahier 1988, pp. 163–4)

2. An interesting example of protection of citizens from the power of the state is the Second Amendment to the Constitution of the United States of America which states: 'A well regulated militia being necessary to the security of a free state, then the right to keep and bear arms shall not be infringed.' This provision was made primarily because the early European settlers, of New England in particular, had a well-founded fear of standing armies, which they saw as instruments which could be seized by monarchs to oppress the people. A *citizen* militia, assembled for specific purposes and then disbanded, did not carry this risk.

   It is a sad irony that in contemporary America, the operation of impeccably democratic institutions allows powerful lobbies such as the American Rifle Association to effectively prohibit gun control – not least by championing this allegedly unqualified constitutional 'right to bear arms'. Here, the working of democratic institutions in a specific historical context denies to American citizens effective protection from terrorists, disturbed teenagers, and others who have repeatedly used freely available automatic weapons for mass murder of their fellow citizens.

3. Hogan's work offers a scholarly and lucid account of the historical development of 'protective citizenship' – which he contrasts with a tradition of 'civic republicanism' deriving ultimately from Aristotle.

4. These issues are examined at length in a challenging but highly illuminating recent book by Eamonn Callan. A fuller discussion of 'public' and 'non-public' values in relation to citizenship is contained in McLaughlin 1992.

Chapter 14

Sex Education

MICHAEL J. REISS

BACKGROUND

The teaching of sex education in schools presents a number of issues. For one thing, whether it should even be taught is questioned by some. Then, the precise aims of sex education vary greatly. Other issues include the age at which school sex education should start, the teaching approaches to be used, the moral framework within which it should take place, the rights of parents to withdraw their children from school sex education, whether classes should (sometimes) be single sex, who should teach it, the training which teachers of sex education should receive, and where within the school curriculum it should be taught. In addition, there are conceptual difficulties in deciding how best to evaluate sex education. This chapter cannot deal with all these issues but focuses on questions of especial importance for those training to be teachers, or teachers early in their teaching career.

SHOULD SEX EDUCATION TAKE PLACE IN SCHOOLS?

UK surveys consistently show that the majority of parents and pupils want sex education to be provided in schools (Ingham 1998). Those who believe that it should not take place in schools generally hold that sex education is the responsibility of parents, and that schools have neither the right nor the competence to teach about it. In particular, those who argue that schools should not teach sex education are frequently unhappy about what they perceive as the amoral, or even immoral, framework adopted by many schools when they do teach sex education.

However, it can be argued that all schools inevitably engage in sex education, simply by their being a community of sexual people each with attitudes and behaviours shaped by their own personal history, by the ethos and composition of the school in which they find themselves and, more generally, by the collective values of the societies in which they grew up and presently exist. What is at debate, if this point of view is accepted, is not whether school sex education should occur, but what sort of sex education should take place.

THE HISTORY OF THE AIMS OF SEX EDUCATION IN THE UK

The history of sex education remains under-researched (Reiss 1998). We know little of school sex education in the UK before the outbreak of the Second World War in 1939, though some work has been done on the oral accounts of adults looking back to their school days as pupils (Humphries 1988). It seems likely that many pupils before the Second World War received little formal school sex education. What there was was probably largely aimed at the prevention of illegitimacy, and sex education at this time seems mainly to have been targeted at girls.

The Second World War had, of course, huge consequences for the lives of most of the population of Europe and a considerable number of countries beyond. It is often the case that the mass movement of people, particularly soldiers, results in an increase in the incidence of sexually transmitted infections. As one might expect, then, the outbreak of the War seems to have resulted in a shift in the main aim of sex education towards the prevention of syphilis and gonorrhoea.

Anecdotal accounts of innumerable lessons on the reproductive systems of rabbits or the pollination habits of flowering plants suggest that much school sex education in the 1950s and 1960s (as must often also have been the case for up to 100 years previously) was largely carried out vicariously through the descriptions, though not the observations, of the reproductive habits of plants and non-human animals. It seems likely that boys, especially if educated in the public school (i.e. private education) boarding system, may also have received warnings about the dangers believed to follow from masturbation.

By the start of the 1970s, school sex education was beginning to change significantly (Went 1995). Biology textbooks started to provide fuller accounts of the human reproductive systems, while methods of contraception began to be taught more widely. The emphasis was mostly on the provision of accurate information, and the aims of sex education programmes included a decrease in ignorance, guilt, embarrassment and anxiety. Issues to do with relationships were probably more often discussed in programmes of personal and social education or their equivalents rather than in biology lessons.

The 1980s continued to see a broadening of the aims of sex education. The growing acceptance of feminist thinking led to an increase in the number of programmes that encouraged pupils to examine the roles played by women and men in society. The aim was typically for students to realize the existence and extent of sexual inequality. Feminist critiques of sex education programmes pointed out how such programmes may simply reinforce gender inequalities (e.g. Wolpe 1987). It began more widely to be appreciated just how gendered was the discourse of sex education, which typically served to perpetuate the belief that male self-control, though possible, could not be relied on and that women by their behaviours should help men to act responsibly (Thomson 1994).

At the same time, sex education programmes increasingly began to have such aims as 'the acquisition of skills for decision-making, communicating, personal relationships, parenting and coping strategies' (Surrey County Council 1987, p. 3). Similar statements are evident in many publications of the time.

As the importance of skills became stressed, so sex education programmes increasingly talked about enabling young people to think for themselves and make their own informed decisions about issues that concerned their sexuality. It was this sort of language that so alarmed many on account of what was perceived as the increasing liberalization of school sex education.

The post-Second World War advent of antibiotics meant that for several decades a fear of sexually transmitted infections played only a minor role in the thinking behind most school sex education programmes. This situation changed suddenly in the late 1980s when it was realized that a new, sexually transmitted agent – human immunodeficiency virus (HIV) – was rapidly spreading in many countries of the world. Near panic set in in some quarters as it began to be appreciated that many, perhaps most, people infected with HIV would go on to develop AIDS and subsequently die, that a person could be infected with HIV and remain thus infectious for many years without realizing it or having any symptoms of infection, and that there was no treatment either for HIV infection or for AIDS itself.

HIV and AIDS became a health issue in the UK at just the time that sex education became a political football. A number of circumstances, including the controversy over the 1985 Gillick case – which focused on whether parents always have the right to know if their children were being issued with contraceptives when under the age of 16 – and the growing strength of the lesbian and gay movement, led to a polarization of views on sex education among politicians at local and national level. A flurry of legislation and government education circulars, which continues to this day, resulted and it increasingly became acknowledged that a values-less sex education programme cannot exist.

Recent school sex education programmes have varied considerably in their aims (Reiss 1993). At one extreme (rarely found in the UK), abstinence education aims to ensure that young people do not engage in heavy petting or sexual intercourse before marriage; on the other hand, some sex education programmes challenge sexist and homophobic attitudes, and try to help young people make their own decisions about their sexual behaviour. Although a plurality of aims in almost any branch of education may be healthy, too great a range of possible aims can confuse both teachers and learners, and in this case may perhaps be indicative of a lack of clarity about the precise functions of sex education.

WHERE IN THE CURRICULUM SHOULD
SCHOOL SEX EDUCATION BE TAUGHT, AND HOW?

Most sex educators agree that the best provision for sex education occurs when schools teach it across the curriculum, in a number of traditional subjects (including Science, English, Religious Studies, History and Geography), in PSE (Personal and Social Education) or PSHE (Personal, Social and Health Education) lessons, and in tutor groups or form periods. Accordingly, all teachers in a school potentially have a role to play in sex education.

Materials used in schools vary greatly in terms of how they treat human sexuality. Some are sensitively written, comprehensive and helpful. Others, though, are sexist, fail to tackle personal issues to do, for example, with menstruation, ignore lesbian and gay issues, and either omit or fail adequately to deal with relevant cultural issues. If you do use published materials to help teach sex education in a secondary school, the most useful 'tip' is probably to get your pupils to critique the materials by discussing among themselves and with you, posing such questions as:

• What useful things do these materials contain?
• What angle do the authors seem to be taking (e.g. 'Don't engage in sexual intercourse until you are ready for it' or 'There is more to sex than sexual intercourse').
• Are there any ways the material could be better? Are there other things which it would have been good for the author to have included?

Published materials can be useful but they shouldn't dominate teaching about sex education. One of the great things about school lessons, when they go well, is that they provide an opportunity for pupils to discuss and reflect on important issues more deeply than they often can outside of school. If you find it difficult to get discussions going, try bringing into school a ten-minute (no longer!) video extract from almost any soap opera and get pupils to discuss various sex-related topics that crop up.

If you are comfortable with role play, this approach can work wonderfully well, especially if pupils are encouraged to play roles different from those that they normally occupy. For instance, pupils (both boys and girls) could role play being young mothers. Often some of the most important learning takes place when pupils are given the chance to talk subsequently about what it felt like to be in role.

A final technique which works well is to get pupils to write anonymous questions which they put into a box at the end of a lesson. This gives you time to think about which ones you want to deal with next lesson and, if needs be, to find someone who can help you answer some of them.

The golden rule for any beginning teacher when teaching sex education is to discuss it first with an appropriate established member of staff (e.g. head of department or head of year). Team teaching may be a possibility if you think that would be helpful. For more extensive guidance about the practicalities of teaching sex education see Massey (1991) and Ray and Went (1995).

THE LEGAL POSITION ABOUT SEX EDUCATION IN UK SCHOOLS

There is, though, much more to successful sex education teaching than following suggestions like those in the previous section. You should know about the legal issues surrounding sex education (this section) and have thought about a moral framework for your teaching (next section).

Unfortunately the recent history of legislation concerning sex education in the UK means that there has been considerable confusion among teachers about what is or is not permitted. A classic instance of this arose in relation to The Local Government Act (50/1) 1988, Section 28 of which states that:

> A local authority shall not – (a) intentionally promote homosexuality or publish material with the intention of promoting homosexuality; (b) promote the teaching in any maintained school of the acceptability of homosexuality as a pretended family relationship by the publication of such material or otherwise.

Many teachers became concerned that they might fall foul of the law simply by *referring* to issues of sexual orientation; other teachers reacted with fury both at the perceived injustice and prejudice, and at the crude assumptions implicit in phraseologies about 'a pretended family relationship'; a minority of teachers welcomed the Circular. However, it then transpired that this part of the Local Government Act (generally referred to as 'Clause 28') did not apply to schools, as Section 18 of the Education Act (No. 2) 1986 – which gave school governors responsibility for decisions on sex education in schools – took precedence.

Section 18 (2) of the Education (N. 2) Act 1986 stipulated that the governing bodies of county, controlled and maintained special schools should consider whether sex education should form part of the secular curriculum for the school. Circular 11/87 stated that

> Teaching about the physical aspects of sexual behaviour should be set within a clear moral framework in which pupils are encouraged to consider the importance of self-restraint, dignity and respect for themselves and others, and helped to recognise the physical, emotional and moral risks of casual and promiscuous sexual behaviour . . . Pupils should be helped to appreciate the benefits of stable married and family life and the responsibilities of parenthood.

This Circular also specified that 'There is no place in any school in any circumstances for teaching which advocates homosexual behaviour, which presents it as the "norm", or which encourages homosexual experimentation by pupils.'

Not surprisingly, Circular 11/87 met with much the same wide range of responses that greeted Section 28 of The Local Government Act (50/1) 1988. However, Circular 11/87 has now been superseded by Circular 5/94 which builds on Section 241 (2) of the Education Act 1993. Though parts of Circular 5/94 have been severely criticized, overall it has been received more positively than Circular 11/87 by organizations which work in the field of school sex education in the UK (e.g. the Sex Education Forum). A key point is that *secondary* schools are required to provide sex education, including education about HIV and AIDS, but parents are given the unequivocal right to withdraw their children from such sex education.

A MORAL FRAMEWORK FOR SEX EDUCATION

Circular 5/94 sets sex education in a 'moral framework', the tone of which is indicated by the following quotation:

> . . . schools' programmes of sex education should therefore aim to present facts in an objective, balanced and sensitive manner, set within a clear framework of values and an awareness of the law on sexual behaviour. Pupils should accordingly be encouraged to appreciate the value of stable family life, marriage and the responsibilities of parenthood. They should be helped to consider the importance of self-restraint, dignity, respect for themselves and others, acceptance of responsibility, sensitivity towards the needs and views of others, loyalty and fidelity. And they should be enabled to recognise the physical, emotional and moral implications, and risks, of certain types of behaviour, and to accept that both sexes must behave responsibly in sexual matters. (Department for Education 1994, p. 6)

While some may be deeply suspicious about such phrases as 'the value of stable family life' and 'the importance of self-restraint', such language is open to profitable discussion and interpretation. Further, the Circular makes no explicit reference to homosexuality. Instead, it simply states that:

> The law does not define the purpose and content of sex education other than declaring that it includes education about HIV and AIDS and other sexually transmitted diseases. In secondary schools sex education should, in the Secretary of State's view, encompass, in addition to facts about human reproductive processes and behaviour, consideration of the broader emotional and ethical dimensions of sexual attitudes . . . (Department for Education 1994. p. 7)

It is difficult to produce a single classification or typology which manages validly to map the various positions that exist with respect to what should be the moral framework for sex education. Two widely used, and useful, classifications are the conservative-v.-liberal one, and the religious-v.-secular one.

The conservative position can be characterized by its belief that what is best can generally be discovered by learning from history. It maintains that traditional values contain much that is valuable, and that if changes are to be made, they should be made slowly and with a high degree of consensus. Further, the conservative position suspects that too high a value can be placed on autonomy, suspecting that one person's autonomy can lead to costly mistakes and much suffering.

The liberal position stands in opposition to the conservative one. A liberal is apt to be sceptical of too great a respect for tradition, holding that a perpetuation of yesterday's values may serve merely to maintain inequalities of power and knowledge. With particular regard to school sex education, a liberal is likely to press for a greater emphasis on individual rights and for more open discussion on such issues as contraception, homosexuality and the roles of men and women.

The secular position (which can be either conservative or liberal) holds that religious values are of little relevance in modern societies. The way forward comes from rational debate unencumbered by religious views which are frequently old-fashioned and unintelligible to most people. An atheist involved in sex education may react with exasperation to theological arguments which are likely to be perceived as being of, at most, marginal relevance for the great majority of people. For example, Roman Catholic agonizings over natural theology and contraception may be considered bizarre and irrelevant.

The religious position (which is often conservative but can be liberal) also holds that rational debate is essential but is less confident about the power of human reason. It maintains that there are other sources of wisdom and knowledge, including those revealed in the scriptures and those discerned by communities of believers and their leaders down the years.

Until recently, little was written on school sex education in the UK from a religious point of view and what there was was largely generated within a mindframe and for an audience which accepted the validity of the religious position. In recent years, though, there has been an increasing acknowledgement from all sex educators, whether or not they themselves are members of any particular religious faith, that the religious point of view needs to be taken into account, if only because a significant number of children and their parents have moral values at least partly informed by religious traditions (Thomson 1993; Reiss and Mabud 1998). Further, it has been argued that religion is increasingly becoming a means through which identities are articulated on the public stage.

TEACHING ABOUT SEXUAL ORIENTATION

Finally, I would like to say a little about one of the most controversial aspects of teaching about sex education, namely whether schools should provide teaching about sexual orientation.

There are a number of reasons that can be put forward in favour of schools teaching explicitly about homosexuality as well as about heterosexuality. First is the argument that the absence of such teaching is deeply hurtful to homosexuals. Adult gays and lesbians, when asked, often tell of the pain they experienced as a result of their apparent non-existence at school, in the structured silence that often surrounds their sexual identity. Not uncommonly, even explicit teacher-controlled discussions on sexuality omit any reference to gay and lesbian orientation and behaviour. There is also evidence that lesbian and gay teenagers are several times more likely both to attempt and to commit suicide than their heterosexual counterparts (Trenchard and Warren 1984) even though lesbian and gay adults probably score at least as well as their heterosexual counterparts on psychological measures of self-esteem (Ruse 1988). It has been suggested that sex education that explicitly addressed issues of sexual orientation might help to reduce the incidence of teenage suicide.

It is difficult to be certain, but a conservative estimate would suggest that at least 4 per cent of adult males and 2 per cent of adult females are exclusively or predominantly homosexual (Johnson *et al.* 1994). In other words, while homosexuals are undeniably a minority, they are a sizeable one – comparable, in the UK, to the number of Muslims or Roman Catholics. As such they deserve the attention and curriculum space when teaching sex education that should be accorded to religious minorities when teaching religious education.

A second argument in favour of teaching about homosexuality is that even if the percentage of people who are exclusively or predominantly homosexual is not large, several times this number have at least some homosexual tendencies, and this may be especially true of teenagers.

A third argument is that all of us, whether or not we are homosexual, need to know about homosexuality in order, as citizens, to understand and be able to make an informed contribution to such questions as 'Should homosexuals be permitted in the Armed Forces?', 'Should the age of consent be the same for homosexuals and heterosexuals?' and 'Should marriage be an option for homosexuals?'

A fourth argument is that such teaching may help to prevent homophobia and reduce the incidence of physical violence experienced by gays and lesbians. A 1994 survey of over 4,200 lesbians, bisexuals and gay men from all over the UK found that 34 per cent of men and 24 per cent of women who took part had experienced violence in the previous five years on account of their sexuality (Mason and Palmer 1996). Teenagers were especially at risk: 48 per cent of respondents under the age of 18 had experienced violence, 61 per cent had been harassed and 90 per cent called names because of their sexuality. While one cannot extrapolate quantitatively from the results of such a survey (over 50,000 copies of the survey were distributed via *Gay Times* and other lesbian and gay publications and databases but with only 8 per cent being returned), the detailed personal accounts nevertheless make harrowing reading.

On the other hand, there are arguments against teaching about homosexuality. One is the belief that such teaching cannot be balanced. Just as Peace Studies and Environmental Education promote peace and the responsible use of the environment, so, it is believed, teaching about homosexuality is likely to lead to its advocacy.

A related fear is that teaching about homosexuality, unless simply to condemn it, results in its implicit legitimization. We do not teach at school in an even-handed way about slavery, murder or child abuse. Indeed, to teach about such issues in a 'balanced' way is wrong, precisely because we hold such behaviours to lie outside the moral pale. Similarly, it can be argued, we should not even help students to consider the arguments in favour of homosexuality.

Further objections are that a significant number of parents do not want their children to be taught about homosexuality, even though other aspects of sex education are widely supported (Ingham 1998) and that many teachers feel uncomfortable teaching about homosexuality.

A different objection is that teaching in this area might even increase homophobia and prejudice. Halstead (1992) argues that three types of controversial issue can be distinguished:

1. Situations where there is agreement over the existence of a particular moral imperative, but disagreement over how to interpret it.
2. Situations where there are conflicting moral imperatives and uncertainty over which should take priority.
3. Situations where disagreement arises because groups do not share the same fundamental moral principles.

Now it isn't always easy to place any particular instance of controversiality into one of these three categories, but it seems likely that the issue of homosexuality may, at least for some people, fall into type (3). The significance of this is that discussion around 'type (3)' controversies may be especially likely to inflame the situation rather than inform the participants. Such discussions may be counterproductive.

While these objections to teaching about homosexuality should not be dismissed, I doubt that they are sufficient, always, to outweigh the arguments in favour. However, to be acceptable, teaching about homosexuality should be:

1. balanced;
2. undertaken only by suitably trained teachers who wish to teach about it;
3. part, where possible, of the explicit curriculum so that parents do not suddenly find that such teaching has been foisted on their children without their being aware of it.

In addition,

4. it should perhaps continue to be the case, as it currently is in England and Wales, that parents have the right to withdraw their children from school sex education (as discussed above);
5. teaching in this area should be evaluated, particularly in terms of its acceptability to those receiving it. If a sex education programme of any sort

proves highly divisive or unacceptable to a significant number, it needs amending.

For further debate about the teaching of sexual orientation in schools, see Reiss (1997), Halstead and Lewicka (1998) and Beck (1999).

CONCLUSION

The above account may have given too much of an impression of the problems that teaching sex education poses. This would be a pity. Most sex education in UK secondary schools isn't very good. Yet good sex education can be extremely valuable. You can provide pupils with accurate information that some of them would otherwise not receive and you can provide a safe framework in which pupils can develop their own views and learn from one another. Finally, don't worry if you feel embarrassed – you probably won't after you have taught the same topic more than a couple of times and, anyway, modesty is a perfectly appropriate virtue. And decline politely to answer any personal questions about your own sexual history.

Chapter 15

Drug Education and Education about Substance Abuse

RUTH JOYCE

THE NATIONAL DRUG STRATEGY AND THE ROLE OF THE EDUCATION SERVICE

Drug use and misuse is part of the history of our civilization. It is a worldwide phenomenon and in the United Kingdom we live in a society where there is widespread use of illegal and legal drugs, both medically and socially. The same drug can kill or cure, depending on how it is used, who uses it and how much is used – alcohol, paracetamol, temazepam and even amphetamines come into this category.

However, even with this long-term perspective in mind, recent studies indicate that there are significant changing patterns of behaviour around drug misuse, especially among young people. In particular:

- Drug misuse is most common among people in their teens and early 20s, but the average use of first drug use is becoming younger.
- Almost half of young people are likely to take drugs at some time in their lives, but only about one-fifth become regular users (i.e. at least once a month) with a tiny minority of that group taking drugs on a daily basis.
- Most young people who use drugs do so out of curiosity, boredom or peer pressure and continue using drugs through a combination of factors ranging from enjoyment to physical and psychological dependency.
- Cannabis is easily the most commonly used drug among the young, followed by amphetamines, poppers, LSD and ecstasy; while there are some identifiable groups such as cannabis users, dance drug users and addicts, the trend is towards more indiscriminate use, based on price and availability.
- There is a very strong correlation between the use of illegal drugs and the use of volatile substances, tobacco and alcohol among young people.
- There is increasingly strong evidence that the earlier a young person starts taking the drugs, the greater the chance that he or she will develop serious drug problems over time.

- From early to mid teens, there are strong links between drug problems, exclusion or truancy from school, break up of the family and initiation into criminal activity.
- For older teenagers and people in their 20s, there are strong links between drug problems and unemployment, homelessness, prostitution and other features of social exclusion.
- Whatever other influences affect young people, the role of parents throughout the process is vital.

All this means that communities, including their schools, have a key role in addressing concerns about the effects of this growing use of legal and illegal drugs. No area in the UK is exempt and the potential and real consequences on the health of our communities, the crime in our communities and the effects it has on individuals and their families, affects us all. This means that we are all having to consider actions to prevent and manage the situations that the changing drug scene presents.

This changing scene led to both national and local responses, with the publication in May 1995 of the then government's three-year strategy 'Tackling Drugs Together'. This first national drug strategy has since been superseded by the recent publication of a ten-year strategy 'Tackling Drugs to Build a Better Britain'. Together, they develop a national framework for action through a series of national plans. These make clear that no single agency carries the responsibility for drug action, but that it is through co-ordinated and coherent action through multi-agency initiatives that we can begin to reduce both the demand and supply, particularly of illegal drugs. It is also acknowledged that a national strategy can only work if it is delivered effectively on the ground. The structure that allows this to happen requires each area to set up a Drugs Action Team (DAT) which includes senior representatives from the police, probation, prison, local authorities – including education – and health authorities. Their main task is to develop and co-ordinate a strategic local plan of action for all services to work together towards common goals.

The role of the education service and schools has been clearly laid out through key documents:

1. *Tackling Drugs Together* (Government White Paper 1995) which stated that schools have an important role in reducing the misuse of drugs and in minimizing their health risks.

   The main objectives in these three areas related to young people are:

   - to discourage young people from taking drugs;
   - to ensure that schools offer effective programmes of drug education;
   - to raise awareness among school staff, governors and parents;
   - to develop effective national and local educational strategies;
   - to ensure that young people at risk of drug misuse or who experiment with or become dependent on drugs have access to a range of advice, counselling, treatment, rehabilitation and aftercare services.

2. *Circular 4/95 Drug Prevention and Schools* (Department for Education 1995) which provides guidance to schools on the drug education curriculum, the principles which should inform it, advice on the policy framework, and advice on ways of handling drug-related incidents in schools. In this respect, it asks that schools should consider the welfare of their pupils and develop a range of appropriate responses to pupil behaviour. It includes the statement that although some behaviour may break the law, it should not automatically lead to pupil exclusion.

3. *Drug Education – Curriculum Guidance for Schools* (School Curriculum and Assessment Authority 1995) which gives more details on the overall approach to drug education in schools. It reinforces the view that:

   - drug education should begin early;
   - it should be delivered within a development framework;
   - it should involve the development of appropriate skills and attitudes as well as transmitting relevant information;
   - it should make use of active teaching and learning styles;
   - it should be developed within a broader whole-school policy on health education and promoting healthy living.

4. *Drug Education and Schools* (Office for Standards in Education 1996). This document also comments on the development of appropriate action in schools. It identifies strengths and weaknesses of practice highlighted by the process of inspection by Ofsted. For the secondary sector, it points out that the poorest level of delivery is typically at Key Stage 3, especially when drug education work is delivered through tutorial sessions, or where it uses strategies which set out to shock or frighten young people. It suggests that the best approaches were those which approached drug education through well-thought-out PSHE programmes. In-service training of teachers is similarly identified as a weak area in those schools where effective dissemination strategies were poorly developed.

5. *The Right Choice – choosing and developing drug education resources for schools* – this booklet, available free to all schools, helps teachers and other school staff decide which materials are most effective.

6. *Tackling Drugs to Build a Better Britain* (Her Majesty's Stationery Office 1998b). The new strategy outlined in this document involves a vision of a healthy and confident society increasingly free from the harm caused to our citizens by the misuse of drugs. It recognizes four elements for action:

   - *Young people* – to help them resist drug misuse in order to achieve their full potential in life.
   - *Communities* – to protect our communities from drug-related antisocial and criminal behaviour.
   - *Treatment* – to enable people with drug problems to overcome them and live healthy, crime-free lives.

- *Availability* – to restrict and control the availability of illegal drugs on our streets.

The broader context of policies to reduce social exclusion and especially school exclusion is addressed, and the agenda for schools is set in the context of a whole range of actions to increase the quality of school delivery in the light of new evidence on effectiveness.

The specific targets for schools will:

- inform young people, parents and those who advise/work with them, about the risks and consequences of drug misuse – including alcohol, tobacco and solvents;
- teach young people from the age of 5 upwards – inside and outside formal education settings – the skills needed to resist pressures to misuse drugs, including a more integrated approach to Personal, Social and Health Education in schools;
- promote healthy lifestyles;
- ensure that young people most at risk have access to specific interventions;
- build on what works best in prevention and education activity.

The increased understanding about the effectiveness of drug education which has been developed as a result of these initiatives is of key importance to school staff. Research suggests that there are nine key factors in effective drug education in school. It should:

1. begin early – in Key Stage 1;
2. include alcohol, tobacco, medicines, solvents as well as illegal drugs within the programme;
3. develop a supportive school ethos – for example, by appointing a co-ordinator, developing a clear and coherent whole-school policy;
4. deliver drug education as part of a broad and developmental PSHE programme;
5. identify and target the needs and understanding of individual young people;
6. use teachers who are both competent and confident in the area as key deliverers;
7. use teaching which focuses on the acquisition of knowledge, the development of skills and the development of appropriate attitudes and values;
8. use interactive/experiential teaching methods;
9. develop the support and commitment of parents and the local community.

Although the strategy does specify what a competent and confident teacher is, there are indicators of competency which should be within all teachers – whether they deliver the curriculum entitlement in the area of drugs education or not.

CONCLUSION: CORE KNOWLEDGE AND SKILLS NEEDED BY SCHOOL STAFF WORKING WITH YOUNG PEOPLE

The following is a summary of the key requirements in this respect. Teachers and other school staff working in this area should have:

- a basic knowledge of the physical, psychological and social effects of drugs;
- a knowledge of the impact on children of substance misuse by parents;
- an awareness of their own attitudes towards and experiences of substance use and how this might affect their work with young people;
- the ability to recognize substance misuse by young people;
- assessment skills, particularly to distinguish between substances used and forms of use, e.g. experimental, recreational and problematic use;
- a knowledge of basic life support skills;
- the capacity to deliver simple interventions, including relevant information and advice;
- information on local agencies and when and how to refer young people appropriately.

Bibliography

Introduction
Beck, J. (1998) *Morality and Citizenship in Education*, London: Cassell.
Cole, M. (ed.) (1999) *Professional Issues for Teachers and Student Teachers*, London: David Fulton.
Cox, C. B. and Dyson, A. E. (1969) *Fight for Education: A Black Paper*, London: The Critical Quarterly Society.
Department for Education and Employment (DfEE) (1998) *Teaching: High Status, High Standards – Requirements for Courses of Initial Teacher Training*, London: DfEE.
Daily Mail (1999) 'Labour drop marriage from morality classes for children: don't mention the M-word', *The Daily Mail*, 14th May.
Hillgate Group (1986) *Whose Schools? A Radical Manifesto*, London: The Hillgate Group.
Norman, E. R. (1977) 'The threat to religion'. In C.B. Cox and R. Boyson (eds) *Black Paper 1977*, London: Maurice Temple Smith, pp. 98–107.
O'Hear, A. (1999) 'Enter the new robot citizens', *The Daily Mail*, 14th May, p. 12.
Qualifications and Curriculum Authority (QCA) and Department for Education and Employment (DfEE) (1999) *The Review of the National Curriculum in England: The Secretary of State's Proposals*, London: QCA and DfEE.
Scruton, R. (1987) 'The myth of cultural relativism'. In E. Palmer (ed.) *Anti-Racism: The Assault on Education and Value*, London: The Sherwood Press.
Weinstock, Sir A. (later, Lord Weinstock) (1976) 'I blame the teachers', *Times Educational Supplement*, 23rd January, p. 12.

Chapter 1
Aldrich, R. (1990) 'The evolution of teacher training'. In N. J. Graves (ed.) *Initial Teacher Education: Policies and Progress*, London: Kogan Page, pp. 12–24.
Aldrich, R. (1996) *Education for the Nation*, London: Cassell.
Batho, G. (1989) *Political Issues in Education*, London: Cassell.
Benn, C. and Simon, B. (1970) *Halfway There*, Harmondsworth: Penguin Books.
Brooks, R. (1991) *Contemporary Debates in Education: An Historical Perspective*, London: Longman.

Department for Education and Employment (1997) *Excellence in Schools,* London: The Stationery Office.

Department for Education and Employment (1998) *News 584/98.*

Gordon, P., Aldrich, R. and Dean, D. (1991) *Education and Policy in England in the Twentieth Century,* London: Woburn Press.

Humphries, S., Mack, J. and Perks, R. (1988) *A Century of Childhood,* London: Sidgwick & Jackson.

Judge, H. (1984) *A Generation of Schooling: English Secondary Schools Since 1944,* Oxford: Oxford University Press.

Lawrence, I. (1992) *Power and Politics at the Department of Education and Science,* London: Cassell.

Lowe, R. (1988) *Education in the Post-war Years: A Social History,* London: Routledge.

Maclure, S. (1970) *A History of Education in London 1870–1990,* Harmondsworth: Penguin Press.

Martin, C. (1979) *A Short History of English Schools,* London: Wayland Publishers.

Sanderson, M. (1999) *Education and Economic Decline in Britain, 1870 to the 1990s,* Cambridge: Cambridge University Press.

Sharp, P. and Dunford, J. (1990) *The Education System in England and Wales,* London: Longman.

Tawney, R. H. (1922) *Secondary Education for All,* London: Allen and Unwin.

Chapter 2

Avis, J. (1996) 'The enemy within: quality and managerialism in education'. In Avis, J., Bloomer, M., Esland, G., Gleeson, D. and Hodkinson, P. *Knowledge and Nationhood: Education, Politics and Work,* London: Cassell.

Bailey, C. H. (1984) *Beyond the Present and the Particular: A Theory of Liberal Education,* especially chs. 4, 7 and 8, London: Routledge & Kegan Paul.

Blair, T. (1998) *The Third Way: New Politics for the New Century,* Fabian Pamphlet 588, London: The Fabian Society.

Bolton, E. (1994) 'Divided we fall', *Times Educational Supplement,* 21st January, p. 7.

Cox, C. B. and Dyson, A. E. (eds) (1969) *Fight for Education: A Black Paper,* London: The Critical Quarterly Society.

Dearing, Sir Ronald (1993) *The National Curriculum and its Assessment – Final Report,* London: School Curriculum and Assessment Authority.

Graham, D. with Tytler, D. (1993) *A Lesson for us All: the Making of the National Curriculum,* London: Routledge.

Gray, J. (1998) *False Dawn: The Delusions of Global Capitalism,* London: Granta Books.

Hargreaves, D. H. (1982) *The Challenge for the Comprehensive School: Culture, Curriculum and Community,* London: Routledge & Kegan Paul.

HEQC (Higher Education Quality Council) (1994) *Choosing to Change: Extending Access, Mobility and Choice in Higher Education (The Robertson Report),* London: HMSO.

Hirst P. H. and Peters R. S. (1970) *The Logic of Education,* London: Routledge & Kegan Paul.

Lawlor, S. (1994) 'This crazy National Curriculum', *The Observer,* 20th February.

Moore, R. (1994) 'Competence, professionality and culture change'. In Wilkin, M. (ed.) *Collaboration and Transition in Initial Teacher Training,* London: Kogan Page.

Norman, E. R. (1977) 'The threat to religion'. In Cox, C. B. and Boyson, R. (eds) *Black Paper 1977,* London: Temple Smith.

O'Hear, P. and White, J. (1993) *Assessing the National Curriculum,* London: Paul Chapman Publishing.

Phillips, M. (1996) *All Must Have Prizes,* London: Little, Brown & Company.

Qualifications and Assessment Authority (QCA) and Department for Education and Employment (DfEE) (1999) *The Review of the National Curriculum in England: The Secretary of State's Proposals,* London: QCA and DfEE.

Scruton, R. (1987) 'The myth of cultural relativism'. In Palmer, E. (ed.) *Anti-racism: The Assault on Education and Value,* London: The Sherwood Press.

Tomlinson, J. (1993) *The Control of Education,* especially chs. 4 and 5, London: Cassell.

Whitty, G. (1990) 'The new Right and the National Curriculum: state control or market forces?' In Flude, M. and Hammer, M. (eds) *The Education Reform Act 1988: Its Origin and Implications,* Basingstoke: The Falmer Press.

Young, M. F. D. (1998) *The Curriculum of the Future: From the 'New Sociology of Education' to a Critical Theory of Learning,* London: Falmer Press.

Chapter 3

Black, P. (1998) *Testing: Friend or Foe? Theory and Practice of Assessment and Testing,* London: Falmer Press.

Black, P. and Wiliam, D. (1998) *Inside the Black Box: Raising Standards Through Classroom Assessment,* London: King's College.

Broadfoot, P. (1996) *Education, Assessment and Society,* Buckingham: Open University Press.

DfEE (1998) *Standards for the Award of Qualified Teacher Status (Annex A of DfEE Circular 4/98).*

Department of Education and Science (1987) *Report of the National Curriculum Task Group on Assessment and Testing,* London: DES.

Gipps, C. (1991) *Assessment: A Teachers' Guide to the Issues,* London: Hodder & Stoughton.

Gipps, C. (1994) *Beyond Testing: Towards a Theory of Educational Assessment,* London: Falmer Press.

Office for Standards in Education (1998) *How teachers Assess the Core Subjects at Key Stage 3,* London: Ofsted.

Rowntree, D. (1977) *Assessing Students: How Shall We Know Them,* London: Harper & Row.

Wood, R. (1991) *Assessment and Testing,* Cambridge: Cambridge University Press.

Chapter 4

Bloom, B. (1976) *Human Characteristics and Social Learning,* New York: McGraw Hill.

Bruner J. S. (1960) *The Process of Education,* Cambridge Mass.: Harvard University Press.

Bruner, J. S. (1966) *Towards a Theory of Instruction,* Cambridge Mass.: Harvard University Press, (paperback, 1968, New York: W. W. Norton Inc.).

Bruner, J. S. (1986) *Actual Minds, Possible Worlds,* Cambridge Mass. and London: Harvard University Press.

Cooper P. and McIntyre, D. (1996)*Effective Teaching and Learning; Teachers' and Students' Perspectives,* Milton Keynes: Open University Press.

De Bono, E. (1995) *Parallel Thinking; From Socrates to de Bono,* Harmondsworth: Penguin Books.

Donaldson, M. (1978) *Children's Minds,* London: Fontana.

Egan, K. (1984) *Educational Development,* Oxford: Oxford University Press.

Entwistle, N. J. (1991) *Styles of Learning and Teaching,* London: Wiley.

Fielding, M. (1996) 'How and why learning styles matter: valuing difference in teachers and learners'. In Hart, S. (ed.) *Differentiation and Equal Opportunities,* London: Routledge.

Holt, J. (1969) *How Children Fail,* New York: Pitman, (UK paperback edition Harmondsworth: Pelican).

Hunt, J. McV. (1961) *Intelligence and Experience,* New York: Ronald Press.

Hunt, J. McV. (1971) 'Using intrinsic motivation to teach young children', *Educational Technology,* Vol. 2, No 2.

Kolb, D. (1984) *Experiential Learning,* Englewood Cliffs: Prentice-Hall.

Kolb, D. (1985) *Learning Style Inventory (Revised Edition),* Boston: McBer.

Lister, I. (1974) *Deschooling: A Reader,* Cambridge: Cambridge University Press.

Neil, A.S. (1960) *Summerhill: A Radical Approach to Child-Rearing,* New York: Hart Publishing Co, (UK paperback edition 1968, Harmondsworth: Pelican Books).

Postman, N. and Weingartner, C. (1969) *Teaching as a Subversive Activity,* New York: Delacorte Press, (UK paperback edition 1971, Harmondsworth: Penguin Books).

Vygotsky, L. S. (1962) *Thought and Language,* Massachusetts: Massachusetts Institute of Technology Press.

Wertsch J. V.(1985) (ed.) *Culture, Communication and Cognition; Vygotskian Perspectives,* Cambridge: Cambridge University Press.

Chapter 5

Advisory Group on Citizenship (1998) *Education for Citizenship and the Teaching of Democracy in Schools,* London: Qualifications and Curriculum Authority: http://www.open.gov.uk/qca/.

Bearne, E. (1998) *Use of Language Across the Secondary Curriculum,* London: Routledge.

Carter, R. (1995) *Keywords in Language and Literacy,* London: Routledge.

Crystal, D. (1996) *Discover Grammar,* London: Longman

DES (1975) *A Language for Life,* London: HMSO.

DES (1989) *English for Ages 5–16,* London: HMSO.

DfEE (1997) *The Implementation of the National Literacy Strategy,* London: HMSO.

DfEE (1998) *The National Literacy Strategy Framework for Teaching,* London: HMSO.

DfEE (1999) *The Review of the National Curriculum in England,* London: QCA.

Edwards, V. (1997) *The Other Languages,* Reading: Reading and Language Information Centre: University of Reading.

Hall, C. and Coles, M. (1999) *Children's Reading Choices,* London: Routledge.

Hall, D. (1995) *Assessing the Needs of Bilingual Learners,* London: David Fulton Publishers.

Kress, G. (1995) *Writing the Future: English and the Making of a Culture of Innovation,* Sheffield: National Association for the Teaching of English.

Meek, M. (ed.) (1996) *Developing Pedagogies in the Multilingual Classroom: The Writings of Josie Levine,* Stoke-on-Trent: Trentham Books.

National Foundation for Educational Research: http://www.nfer.ac.uk/.

National Literacy Trust: http://www.literacytrust.org.uk/.

National Writing Project (1990) *Ways of Looking,* London: Nelson.

Norman, K. (ed.) (1992) *Thinking Voices,* London: Hodder & Stoughton.

Perera, K. (1987) *Understanding language,* National Association for the Advancement of Education.

Sainsbury, M. *et al*. (1997) *Evaluation of Summer Literacy Schools,* National Foundation of Educational Research (NFER).
Sampson, G. (1925) *English for the English,* Cambridge: Cambridge University Press.
SCAA (1997a) *Use of Language: A Common Approach,* London: SCAA.
SCAA (1997b) *Extended Writing in Key Stage 3 History,* London: SCAA.
Vygotsky, L.S. (1978) *Mind in Society,* Cambridge, Massachusetts and London: Harvard.
Vygotsky, L.S. (1986) *Thought and Language,* Cambridge, Massachusetts and London: Massachusetts Institute of Technology.
Wray, D. and Lewis, M. (1997) *Extending Literacy,* London: Routledge.

Chapter 6
Berthoud, J. (1996) *Pecking Order,* London: Victor Gollancz.
Best, R., Lang, P., Lodge, C. and Watkins, C. (1995) *Pastoral Care and Personal-Social Education,* London: Cassell.
Blackburn, K. (1975) *The Tutor,* London: Heinemann.
Bradley, J. and Dubinsky, H. (1994) *Understanding 15–17 Year Olds,* London: Rosendale Press.
Conger, J. J. and Petersen, A. C. (1984) *Adolescence and Youth: Psychological Development in a Changing World,* London: Harper & Row.
Erikson, E. H. (1963) *Childhood and Society,* London: Paladin, Granada.
Erikson, E. H. (1984) 'Adolescence'. In Conger, J. J. and Petersen, A. C. (eds) *Adolescence and Youth,* New York: Harper & Row.
Fontana, D. (1981) *Psychology for Teachers,* London: Macmillan.
Francis, L. J. and Kay, W. K. (1994) *Teenage Religion and Values,* Gracewing.
Frankel, R. (1998) *The Adolescent Psyche,* London: Routledge.
Goleman, D. (1996) *Emotional Intelligence,* London: Bloomsbury.
McLaughlin, C., Clark, P. and Chisholm, M. (1996) *Counselling and Guidance in Schools,* London: David Fulton.
McLaughlin, T. H, (1994) 'Values, coherence and the school', *Cambridge Journal of Education*, 24, 3
Malsow, A. (1984) In Conger, J. J. and Petersen, A.C., *op. cit.*
Marland, M. (1989) *The Tutor and the Tutor Group,* London: Longman.

Chapter 7
Audit Commission (1992a) *Getting in on the Act,* London: HMSO.
Audit Commission (1992b) *Getting the Act Together,* London: HMSO.
Black, P. (1996) 'Formative assessment and the improvement of learning', *British Journal of Special Education*, 23, 2, pp. 51–5.
Department for Education (1994) *The Code of Practice on the Identification and Assessment of Special Educational Needs,* London: DFE.
Department for Education and Employment (1998) *Special Educational Needs: A Programme for Action,* London: The Stationery Office.
Department for Education and Science (1978) *Special Educational Needs (The Warnock Report),* London: HMSO.
Florian, L. and Rouse, M. (1999) *Inclusive Practice in Secondary Classrooms: Report to the Research and Development Fund,* Cambridge: University of Cambridge School of Education.
Hart, S. (1996) *Beyond Special Needs: Enhancing Children's Learning Through Innovative Thinking,* London: Paul Chapman

Lewis, A. (1995) (2nd edn) *Primary Special Needs and the National Curriculum*, London: Routledge.

Lewis, A. (1996) 'Summative National Curriculum assessments of primary aged children with special needs', *British Journal of Special Education*, 23, 4, pp. 9–14.

McLaughlin, M. and Tilstone, C. (1999) 'Standards and the curriculum: the core of educational reform'. In McLaughlin, M. and Rouse, M., *Special Education and School Reform in the United States and Britain*, London: Routledge.

Rouse, M. and Agbenu, R. (1998) 'Assessment and special educational needs: teachers' dilemmas', *British Journal of Special Education*, 25, 2, pp. 81–7

Wedell, K. (1990) 'Overview: the 1988 Act and current principles of special educational needs', in Daniels, H. and Ware, J. (eds) *Special Educational Needs and the National Curriculum*, London: Kogan Page.

Wedell, K., Evans, J., Goacher, B. and Welton, J. (1987) 'The 1981 Education Act: policy and provision for special educational needs', *British Journal of Special Education*, 14, 2, pp. 50–3.

Chapter 8

Abraham, J. (1995) *Divide and School: Gender and Class Dynamics in Comprehensive Education*, London: Falmer Press.

Arnot, M., David, M. and Weiner, G. (1996) *Educational Reforms and Gender Equality in Schools*, Manchester: Equal Opportunities Commission.

Arnot, M., Gray. J., James, M. and Rudduck, J. (1998) *Recent Research on Gender and Educational Performance*, London: Ofsted/The Stationery Office.

Arnot, M., David, M. and Weiner, G. (1999) *Closing the Gender Gap: Post-war Social and Educational Change*, Oxford: Polity Press.

Basit, T. B. (1997) *Eastern Values, Western Milieu: Identities and Aspirations of Adolescent Muslim Girls*, Aldershot: Ashgate.

Bastiani, J. (1997) *Home and School in Multicultural Settings: A Working Alliance*, London: Fulton.

Blair, M. and Bourne J. with Coffin, C., Creese, A. and Kenner, C. (1998) *Making the Difference; Teaching and Learning Strategies in Successful Multi-ethnic Schools*, Sudbury: DfEE Publications.

Bleach, K. (ed.) (1998) *Raising Boys' Achievement in Schools*, Stoke on Trent: Trentham Books.

Bray, R., Downes, P., Gardner, C., Hannan, G. and Parsons, N. (1997) *Can Boys Do Better?* Leicester: Secondary Heads Association.

Callender, C. (1997) *Education and Empowerment: The Practice and Philosophies of Black Teachers*, Stoke on Trent: Trentham Books.

Channer, Y. (1995) *I am a Promise; The School Achievement of British African Caribbeans*, Stoke on Trent: Trentham.

Chaplain, R. (1996) 'Making a strategic withdrawal: disengagement and self-worth protection in male pupils'. In Rudduck, J. Chaplain, R. and Wallace, G. (eds) *School Improvement; What Can Pupils Tell Us?* London: David Fulton.

Connolly, P. (1998) *Racism, Gender Identities and Young Children: Social Relations in a Multi-ethnic Inner-city Primary School*, London: Routledge.

Epstein, D., Elwood, J., Hey, V. and Maw, J. (eds) (1998) *Failing Boys? Issues in Gender and Achievement*, Buckingham: Open University.

Gilbert, R. and Gillborn, P. (1998) *Masculinity Goes to School*, London: Routledge.

Gillborn, D. (1995) *Racism and Anti-racism in Real Schools*, Buckingham: Open University Press.

Gillborn, D. (1997) 'Young black and failed by school: the market, education reform and black students', *International Journal of Inclusive Education*, 1, 1, pp. 65–87.

Gillborn, D. and Gipps, C. (1996) *Recent Research on the Achievements of Ethnic Minority Pupils*, London: Ofsted/HMSO.

Kenway, J. and Willis, S. (1998) *Answering Back: Girls, Boys and Feminism in Schools*, London: Routledge.

Mac an Ghaill, M. (1994) *The Making of Men: Masculinities, Sexualities and Schooling*, Buckingham: Open University Press.

MacDonald, A., Saunders, L. and Benfield, P. (1999) *Boys' Achievement: Progress, Motivation and Participation. Issues Raised by the Recent Literature*, Slough: NFER.

MacPherson, Sir William (1999) *The Stephen Lawrence Inquiry. Report of an Inquiry*, London: The Stationery Office.

Mirza, H. S. (1992) *Young, Female and Black*, London: Routledge.

National Commission on Education (1993) *Learning to Succeed: A Radical Look at Education Today and a Strategy for the Future*, London: Heinemann.

Office for Standards in Education (1999) *Raising the Attainment of Minority Ethnic Pupils: School and LEA Responses*, London: Ofsted.

Rolfe, H. (1999) *Gender Equality and the Careers Service*, Manchester: Equal Opportunities Commission.

Runnymede Trust (1998) *Improving Practice: A Whole School Approach to Raising the Achievement of African Caribbean Youth*, (with Weekes, D. and Wright, C.), London: Runnymede Trust.

Sewell, T. (1997) *Black Masculinities and Schooling*, Stoke on Trent: Trentham Books.

Swann, Lord (1985) *Education for All: Final Report of the Committee of Inquiry into the Education of Children from Ethnic Minority Groups*, Cmnd 9453, London: HMSO.

Teese, R., Davies, M., Charlton, M. and Polesel, J. (1995) *Who Wins at School? Boys and Girls in Australian Secondary Education*, Department of Education, Policy and Management: University of Melbourne.

Troyna, B. and Hatcher, R. (1992) *Racism in Children's Lives*, London: Routledge.

Wright, C., Weekes, D., McLaughlin, A. and Webb, D. (1998) 'Masculinised discourses within education and the construction of black male identities amongst African-Caribbean youths', *British Journal of Sociology of Education.*, 19, 1, pp. 75–87.

Chapter 9

Bailey, C. (1984) *Beyond the Present and the Particular. A Theory of Liberal Education*, London: Routledge & Kegan Paul.

Bridges, D. and McLaughlin, T. H. (eds) (1994) *Education and the Market Place*, London: Falmer Press.

Feinberg, J. (1980) 'The child's right to an open future'. In Aiken, W. and LaFollette, H. (eds) *Whose Child? Children's Rights, Parental Authority, and State Power*, Totowa NJ: Littlefield Adams & Co.

Jonathan, R. (1997) *Illusory Freedoms. Liberalism, Education and the Market*, Oxford: Blackwell.

McLaughlin, T. H. (1992) 'The ethics of separate schools'. In Leicester, M. and Taylor, M. (eds) *Ethics, Ethnicity and Education*, London: Kogan Page.

McLaughlin, T. H. (1994a) 'The scope of parents' educational rights' in Halstead, J. M. (ed.) *Parental Choice and Education: Principles, Policy and Practice*, London: Kogan Page.

McLaughlin, T. H. (1994b) 'Politics, markets and schools: the central issues'. In Bridges,

D. and McLaughlin, T. H. (eds) *Education and the Market Place*, London: Falmer Press.

Midwinter, E. (1975) *Education and the Community,* London: Unwin.

Ree, H. (1973) *Educator Extraordinary: The Life and Achievement of Henry Morris*, London: Longman.

Tooley, J. (1996) *Education Without the State,* London: The Education and Training Unit, The Institute of Economic Affairs

White, J. (1990) *Education and the Good Life. Beyond the National Curriculum,* London: Kogan Page

Chapter 10

Bonnett, M. (1997) 'Environmental education and beyond', *Journal of Philosophy of Education*, 31, pp. 249–66.

Corney, G. and Middleton, N. (1996) 'Teaching environmental issues in schools and higher education'. In Rawling, E. M. and Daugherty, R. A. (eds) *Geography into the Twenty-First Century,* Chichester: Wiley, pp. 321–38.

Corney, G. (1998) 'Learning to teach environmental issues', *International Research in Geographical and Environmental Education*, 7, 2, pp. 90–105.

Dove, J. (1996) 'Student teachers' understanding of the greenhouse effect, ozone layer depletion and acid rain', *Environmental Education Research*, 2, 10, pp. 89–100.

Fien, J. (1995) 'Teaching for a sustainable world: the environmental and development education project for teacher education', *Environmental Education Research*, 1, 1, pp. 21–33.

Fien, J. and Slater, F. (1985) 'Four strategies for values education in geography. In Boardman, D. (ed.) *New Directions in Geographical Education,* Lewes: Falmer Press, pp. 171–86.

Gayford, C. (1991) 'Environmental education: a question of emphasis in the school curriculum', *Cambridge Journal of Education*, 21, 1, pp. 73–93.

Hicks, D. (1994) *Education for the Future: A Practical Classroom Guide,* Godalming: Worldwide Fund for Nature.

Hicks, D. and Holden, C. (1995) Exploring the Future: A Missing Dimension in Environmental Education, *Environmental Education Research*, 1, 2, pp. 185–93.

Huckle, J. (1990) 'Environmental education : teaching for a sustainable future'. In Dufour, B. (ed.) *The New Social Curriculum: A Guide to Cross-curricular Issues,* Cambridge: Cambridge University Press, Ch. 10.

Huckle, J. (1993a) 'Environmental education and sustainability: a view from critical theory', Ch. 3. In Fien, J. (ed.) *Environmental Education: A Pathway to Sustainability*, Geelong: Deakin University Press.

Huckle, J. (1993b) 'Environmental education and the National Curriculum in the United Kingdom', *International Research in Geographical and Environmental Education*, 2, 2, pp. 101–4.

Huckle, J., Allen, E., Edwards, P., Symons, G. and Webster, K. (1995) *Reaching Out: Education for Sustainability*, Godalming: Worldwide Fund for Nature.

Naish, M., Rawling, E. M. and Hart, C. (1987) *Geography 16–19: the Contribution of a Curriculum Development Project to 16–19 Education*, Harlow: Longman.

National Curriculum Council (1990) *Curriculum Guidance 7: Environmental Education*, York: National Curriculum Council.

Pike, G. and Selby, D. (1988) *Global Teacher, Global Learner,* London: Hodder and Stoughton.

Stenhouse, L. (1970) *The Humanities Project: An Introduction,* London: Heinemann.

Sterling, S. (1993) 'Environmental education and sustainability: a view from holistic ethics'. In Fien, J. (ed.) *Environmental Education: A Pathway to Sustainability*, Geelong: Deakin University Press.

Sterling, S. and the Edet Group (1992) *Good Earth-Keeping: Education, Training and Awareness for a Sustainable Future*, Environment and Development Education and Training Group, London: UNEP-UK.

Tilbury, D. (1995) 'Environmental education for sustainability: defining the new focus of environmental education in the 1990s', *Environmental Education Research*, 1, 2, pp. 195–212.

United Nations Conference on Environment and Development (1992) *Earth Summit '92*, Ch. 36, Conches: UNCED.

Ward, C. and Fyson, A. (1973) *Streetwork: the Exploding School*, London: Routledge & Kegan Paul.

World Commission on Environment and Development (1987) *Our Common Future*, London: WCED.

Chapter 11

Bottery, M. (1990) *The Morality of the School: The Theory and Practice of Values in Education*, London: Cassell.

Bridges, D. (1986) 'Dealing with controversy in the school curriculum: a philosophical perspective'. In Wellington, J. J. (ed.) *Controversial Issues in the Curriculum*, Oxford: Basil Blackwell.

Great Britain, House of Commons (1985) *Education for All. The Report of the Committee of Inquiry into the Education of Children from Ethnic Minority Groups*, cmnd. 9453, London: HMSO.

Halstead, J. M. and Taylor, M. J. (eds) (1996) *Values in Education and Education in Values*, London: Falmer Press.

Haydon, G. (1997) *Teaching About Values: A New Approach*, London: Cassell.

McLaughlin, T. H. (1992) 'The ethics of separate schools'. In Leicester, M. and Taylor, M. J. (eds) *Ethics, Ethnicity and Education*, London: Kogan Page.

McLaughlin, T. H. (1995a) 'Public values, private values and educational responsibility'. In Pybus, E. and McLaughlin, T. H. *Values, Education and Responsibility*, St Andrews, Centre for Philosophy and Public Affairs: University of St Andrews.

McLaughlin, T. H. (1995b) 'Liberalism, education and the common school' *Journal of Philosophy of Education*, 29, pp. 239–55.

Qualifications and Curriculum Authority (1998) *Education for Citizenship and the Teaching of Democracy in Schools. Final Report of the Advisory Group on Citizenship*, London: Qualifications and Curriculum Authority.

Sacks, J. (1991) *The Persistence of Faith. Religion, Morality and Society in a Secular Age. The Reith Lectures 1990*, London: Weidenfeld & Nicolson.

White, J. (1990) *Education and the Good Life. Beyond the National Curriculum*, London: Kogan Page.

Chapter 12

Best, R. and Lang, P. (1997) 'Introduction'. In Haydon, G. *Teaching About Values*, London: Cassell.

Cohen, B. (1969) 'The problem of bias'. In Heater, D. (ed.) *The Teaching of Politics*, London: Methuen.

Haydon, G. (1997) *Teaching About Values*, London: Cassell.

Hirst, P. (1973) 'The foundations of moral judgement'. In Lord, E. and Bailey, C. (eds)

A Reader in Religious and Moral Education, London: SCM.

Kohlberg, L. (1966) 'Moral education in the schools: a developmental view', *School Review*, pp.1–30.

Kohlberg, L. (1969) 'Stage and sequence: the cognitive developmental approach to socialization', in Goslin, D. (ed.) *Handbook of Socialization Theory and Practice,* Chicago: Rand McNally.

National Forum for Values in Education and the Community (1996) *Consultation on Values in Education and the Community,* London: School Curriculum and Assessment Authority.

Pring, R. (1987) *Personal and Social Education in the Curriculum,* London: Hodder & Stoughton.

Spiecker, B. (1988) 'Education and the moral emotions'. In Spiecker, B. and Straughan, R. (eds) *Philosophical Issues in Moral Education and Development,* Milton Keynes: Open University Press.

Straughan, R. (1982) *Can We Teach Children to be Good?,* London: George Allen & Unwin.

Talbot, M. and Tate, N. (1997) 'Shared values in a pluralist society'. In Smith, R. and Standish, P. (eds) *Teaching Right and Wrong,* Stoke on Trent: Trentham Books.

Warnock, M. (1996) 'Moral values'. In Halstead, J. M. and Taylor, M. J. (eds) *Values in Education and Education in Values,* London: Falmer Press.

White, J. (1994) 'Instead of Ofsted', *Cambridge Journal of Education,* 24, 3, pp. 369–77.

Wringe, C. (1998) 'Reasons, rules and virtues in moral education', in *Journal of Philosophy of Education,* 32, pp. 225–37.

Chapter 13

Advisory Group on Citizenship (1998) *Education for Citizenship and the Teaching of Democracy in Schools: Final Report of the Advisory Group on Citizenship,* London: Department for Education and Employment and The Qualifications and Curriculum Authority.

Ahier, J. (1988) *Industry, Children and the Nation: An Analysis of National Identity in School Textbooks,* London: Falmer Press.

Aristotle (1981) *The Politics,* (revised edn, (ed.) Saunders, T. J.), Harmondsworth: Penguin.

Beck, J. (1998) *Morality and Citizenship in Education,* London: Cassell.

Callan, E. (1997) *Creating Citizens: Political Education and Liberal Democracy,* Oxford: Clarendon Press.

Commission on Citizenship (1990) *Encouraging Citizenship (Report of the House of Commons Commission on Citizenship),* London: HMSO.

Dahrendorf, R. (1996) 'Citizenship and social class'. In Bulmer, M. and Rees, A. M. (eds) *Citizenship Today: The Contemporary Relevance of T. H. Marshall,* London: University College London Press.

Fogelman, K. (1997) 'Citizenship education in England'. In Kennedy, K. (ed.) *Citizenship Education and the Modern State,* London: Falmer Press.

Gellner, E. (1992) *Reason and Culture: The Historic Role of Rationality and Rationalism,* Oxford: Blackwell.

Gilbert, R. (1997) 'Issues for citizenship in a postmodern world'. In Kennedy, K. (ed.) *Citizenship and the Modern State,* London: Falmer Press.

Hogan, D. (1997) 'The logic of protection: citizenship, justice and political community'. In Kennedy, K. (ed.) *Citizenship Education and the Modern State,* London: Falmer Press.

Hurd, D. (1988) 'Citizenship in the Tory democracy', *New Statesman,* 29th April.

McLaughlin, T. H. (1992) 'Citizenship, diversity and education: a philosophical perspective', *Journal of Philosophy of Education,* 29, 2, pp. 239–50.

Marshall, T. H. (1950) *Citizenship and Social Class,* Cambridge: Cambridge University Press.

Marshall, T. H. (1964) 'Citizenship and social class'. In Marshall, T., *Class, Citizenship and Social Development,* Chicago: Chicago University Press.

Ministry of Education (1949) *Citizens Growing Up,* Pamphlet No. 16, London: Ministry of Education.

Moore, R. and Muller, J. (1999) 'The discourse of 'voice' and the problem of identity in the sociology of education', *British Journal of Sociology of Education,* 20, 2.

National Curriculum Council (1990) *Curriculum Guidance 8: Education for Citizenship,* London: National Curriculum Council.

Qualifications and Assessment Authority (QCA) and Department for Education and Employment (DfEE) (1999) *The Review of the National Curriculum in England: The Secretary of State's Proposals,* London: QCA and DfEE.

Rawls, J. (1993) *Political Liberalism,* New York: Columbia University Press.

Taylor, C. (1989) 'Cross-purposes: the liberal-communitarian debate'. In Rosenblum, N. (ed.) *Liberalism and the Moral Life,* Cambridge Mass.: Harvard University Press, pp. 159–82.

Chapter 14

Beck, J. (1999) 'Should homosexuality be taught as an acceptable alternative lifestyle? A Muslim perspective: a response to Halstead and Lewicka', *Cambridge Journal of Education,* 29, pp. 121–30.

Department for Education (1994) *Circular 5/94 – Sex Education in Schools,* London: Department for Education.

Halstead, J. M. (1992) 'Ethical dimensions of controversial events in multicultural education'. In Leicester, M. and Taylor, M. (eds), *Ethics, Ethnicity and Education,* London: Kogan Page, pp. 39–56.

Halstead, J. M. and Lewicka, K. (1998) 'Should homosexuality be taught as an acceptable alternative lifestyle? A Muslim perspective', *Cambridge Journal of Education,* 28, pp. 49–64.

Humphries, S. (1988) *A Secret World of Sex,* London: Sidgwick & Jackson.

Ingham, R. (1998) *Exploration of the Factors that Affect the Delivery of Sex and Sexuality Education and Support in Schools: Final Report to the former Wessex Region NHS R and D Sexual Health Taskforce,* Southampton: Centre for Sexual Health Research, Faculty of Social Sciences, University of Southampton.

Johnson, A. M., Wadsworth, J., Wellings, K. and Field, J. (1994) *Sexual Attitudes and Lifestyles,* Oxford: Blackwell Scientific Publications.

Mason, A. and Palmer, A. (1996) *Queerbashing: A National Survey of Hate Crimes against Lesbians and Gay Men,* London: Stonewall.

Massey, D. (1991, 2nd edn) *School Sex Education: Why, What and How,* London: Family Planning Association.

Ray, C. and Went, D. (1995) *Good Practice in Sex Education: A Sourcebook for Schools,* London: Sex Education Forum / National Children's Bureau.

Reiss, M. (1993) 'What are the aims of school sex education?', *Cambridge Journal of Education,* 23, pp. 125–36.

Reiss, M. J. (1997) 'Teaching about homosexuality and heterosexuality', *Journal of Moral Education,* 26, pp. 343–52.

Reiss, M. J. (1998) 'The history of school sex education', *Muslim Education Quarterly,*

15, 2, pp. 4–13.

Reiss, M. J. and Mabud, S. A. (eds) (1998) *Sex Education and Religion*, Cambridge: The Islamic Academy.

Ruse, M. (1988) *Homosexuality: A Philosophical Inquiry*, Oxford: Basil Blackwell.

Surrey County Council (1987) *Sex Education: A Guide for Schools/Colleges*, Woking: Surrey County Council.

Thomson, R. (ed.) (1993) *Religion, Ethnicity and Sex Education: Exploring the Issues*, London: National Children's Bureau.

Thomson, R. (1994) 'Moral rhetoric and public health pragmatism: the recent politics of sex education', *Feminist Review*, 48, pp. 40–59.

Trenchard, L. and Warren, H. (1984) *Something to Tell You*, London: Gay Teenagers' Group.

Went, D. (1995) 'From biology to empowerment: how notions of good practice have changed', Paper presented on 11 July, Copthorne Tara Hotel, London at the 'Sex Education in Schools: Working towards Good Practice' Conference.

Wolpe, A-M (1987) 'Sex in schools: back to the future', *Feminist Review*, 27, pp. 37–47.

Chapter 15

Davies, J. and Coggens, N. (1991) *The Facts about Adolescent Drug Abuse*, London: Cassell.

Department for Education and Employment (1995) *Circular 4/95 – Drug Prevention and Schools*, London: DfEE.

Department for Education and Employment and The School Curriculum and Assessment Authority (1995) *Drug Education – Curriculum Guidance for Schools*, London: DfEE.

Health Education Authority (1995) *A Parents' Guide to Drugs and Solvents*, London: Health Education Authority.

Her Majesty's Stationery Office (1990) *The Need for a New Impetus – Drug Education and Schools*, ACMD.

Her Majesty's Stationery Office (1998a) *Drug Misuse and the Environment*, ACMD.

Her Majesty's Stationery Office (1998b) *Tackling Drugs to Build a Better Britain*, London: HMSO.

ISDD (1997) *Drug Abuse Briefing – 6*.

ISDD (1997) *Drug Misuse in the UK*.

Joyce, R. and Grant, R. (1997) *Smack or Sympathy – Exploring Drug Issues in Schools*, London: Forbes.

Office for Standards in Education (1996) *Drug Education and Schools*, London: Ofsted.

Parker, H. (1995) *Drug Futures: Changing Patterns of Drug Use amongst English Youth*.

SCODA (1998) *The Right Choice – Choosing Drug Education Resources*.

Index